Mutiny or Murder?

Mutiny or Murder?

THE BLOODSOAKED VOYAGE OF THE *CHAPMAN* CONVICT SHIP

CONOR REIDY

The
History
Press
Ireland

Dedicated to my wife Kathleen

Front cover: Unfortunately there are no images of the *Chapman* that reflect the turmoil of the voyage as effectively as the one on the front cover. This ship, the *Lady Blackwood*, is a slightly later model than the *Chapman*, but is from the same era and very similar in make and design.

First published 2018

The History Press Ireland
50 City Quay
Dublin 2
Ireland
www.thehistorypress.ie

© Conor Reidy, 2018

The right of Conor Reidy to be identified as the Author
of this work has been asserted in accordance with the
Copyright, Designs and Patents Act 1988.

British Library Cataloguing in Publication Data.
A catalogue record for this book is available from the British Library.

ISBN 978 0 7509 8564 2

Typesetting and origination by The History Press
Printed in Great Britain

Contents

About the Author

DR CONOR REIDY is a specialist in Irish penal and criminal history. He holds a PhD from the University of Limerick and a BA from NUI Galway. He has held lecturing positions at the University of Limerick and Mary Immaculate College Limerick. His previously published books include *Criminal Irish Drunkards* and *Ireland's 'Moral Hospital':The Irish Borstal System 1906-1956*. He is the author of numerous chapters in edited volumes on subjects including juvenile crime, alcoholism and criminality, and gender history. He has appeared many times in local and national media in Ireland including on RTE Radio, TG4 and Newstalk. Dr Reidy is a former Honorary Secretary of the Women's History Association of Ireland and now works full-time as a freelance editor.

Acknowledgements

I extend my gratitude to the organisations and individuals who, through their efficiency and creativity, preserved and provided the source material upon which this book is based. These include the National Archives of Ireland, State Library of New South Wales and the National Maritime Museum at Greenwich.

I would like to thank my friend and colleague Dr Mary McCarthy for introducing me to Australian history ten years ago and ultimately encouraging me to write what is, for me, a very different type of book. I also thank her and Michael Roycroft for reading early drafts of various chapters. Naturally, any errors, omissions or inaccuracies are mine only. I sincerely appreciate the support of The History Press Ireland, particularly Ronan Colgan and Nicola Guy, for putting faith in my work once again.

As always, a number of friends and family have provided a world of moral support along the way. Special thanks to Edel and Kevin Copeland, Brendan Murphy, Ellen Murphy, Gerard and Heather Reidy, Maura Reidy, and Michael, Ellen and Cáit Healy. To the May 2010 Club, thank you! I am deeply indebted to my cousin Michelle Duckett for always providing a much-needed boost of confidence.

I continue to be inspired by the strength and courage of my parents, John and Betty Reidy, and I thank them for always promoting the importance of the written word from the beginning.

Once again, I could only make this happen with the support of my greatest champion and source of strength. I reserve my warmest thanks to my wife Kathleen for her boundless patience, belief and great humour.

Chronology

13 May 1787	The First Fleet departs from Portsmouth bound for New South Wales
10 April 1791	The *Queen* is the first convict transport to leave Ireland for Australia
1 January 1810	Lachlan Macquarie sworn in as governor of New South Wales
28 November 1816	Alexander Dewar is appointed surgeon-superintendent of the *Chapman*
11 December 1816	The *Chapman* departs the naval dockyard at Deptford
9 January 1817	The *Chapman* arrives at the Cove of Cork
5 February 1817	The first convicts board the ship
15 March 1817	The *Chapman* departs Ireland for New South Wales
22 March 1817	Soldiers and crew are called to arms as a result of a false alarm on deck
4 April 1817	The ship anchors in Porto Praya
7 April 1817	The *Chapman* resumes the journey to New South Wales
17 April 1817	A prolonged shooting incident leaves several convicts dead in the evening

18 April 1817	Three convicts are discovered dead from the shooting; twenty-two wounded
21 April 1817	Convict Thomas Mulholland dies from his wounds
23 April 1817	Convict James Roberts dies from his wounds
25 April 1817	Convict Daniel Parker dies from his wounds
27 April 1817	Soldiers and crew are called to arms following a false alarm
28 April 1817	A second gunfire incident is launched, killing the convict John McArdell
28 April 1817	In a separate incident, convict Bryan Kelly is shot on the poop deck
28 April 1817	Convict Oliver Wallace dies from his wounds in the first shooting episode
5 May 1817	In the worst day of mass punishments on the voyage, fifteen prisoners are flogged
25 May 1817	Sailor Francis Lucy dies following a shooting against the jolly boat
26 May 1817	Convict John Malone dies from gunshot wounds in an earlier incident
29 May 1817	Convict John Jackson dies from wounds sustained in the jolly boat shooting
29 May 1817	Convict James Collins dies from unspecified causes
27 June 1817	Convict Christopher Kelly dies from unspecified causes
27 July 1817	The *Chapman* arrives at Port Jackson, New South Wales
31 July 1817	Colonial Secretary John Campbell begins a routine inspection of the *Chapman*
2 August 1817	Campbell notifies Captain Drake of his intention to pursue criminal charges
8 August 1817	The register of the *Chapman* is seized by the New South Wales government
13 August 1817	Governor Macquarie signs warrant appointing a committee of inquiry

16 August 1817	The Wylde–Wentworth–Campbell committee begins investigations
15 November 1817	Wentworth, Wylde and submit their reports to Governor Macquarie
21 December 1817	The *Chapman* departs New South Wales for India
22 December 1817	The *Harriet* departs New South Wales for London
11 January 1819	Clements and Drake appear at the Admiralty Sessions at the Old Bailey
12 January 1819	Drake, Dewar and Busteed appear at the Admiralty Sessions
12 April 1819	Governor Macquarie is reprimanded by the London government

Preface

The first course I taught during my former career as a university lecturer was the history of modern Australia. One of the first things I was confronted with was the fact that a belief once existed among historians that Australian history begins in 1776 or 1788. Knowing that human beings walked on that continent for more than 40,000 years discredits that notion as a fantasy that was probably driven by some motivation other than the promotion of historical accuracy. To study the modern history of Australia, however, is to witness what was arguably one of the most audacious feats of nation-building that has been undertaken by human beings in the past 250 years. What began as a collection of flimsy wooden shacks constructed on the banks of Botany Bay by the first European settlers who landed in 1788 went on to become a fully functioning world power by the beginning of the twentieth century. Teaching the history of this achievement, I was confronted with the obvious fact that my own core research interest was the key driver of this new colonial society and its economy for the first several decades.

When we take a step back and examine the broader scenario we can appreciate the complex thought processes that went into using the detection and punishment of everyday crime in one part of the world as a means of populating a vast land mass many thousands of miles away. My academic career has been built on the study of crime and its punishment, and I have long been particularly interested in understanding prison reform and the evolution of the penal process. Transportation to Australia was a new concept when it began at the end of the 1780s. Transportation as a means of punishment was not new, however, with the American colonies having provided a useful dumping ground long before Captain Cook sighted Botany Bay.

In taking this first step into the study of Australian history I am not so much concerned with the development of those early colonies – something that continues to be examined most effectively by many others – as I am with the vehicle of transportation. This book has its genesis in a chance discovery at the National Archives of Ireland. Buried in the developing catalogue of the Chief Secretary's Office Registered Papers was an obscure letter to an official in Dublin Castle from some unknown figure in the government of New South Wales. The letter mentioned two villainous convicts on the transportation ship the *Chapman* and their scheme to sow discontent on the journey to New South Wales by spreading false tales of a planned prisoner mutiny. The consequence of this was the death of twelve prisoners and the wounding of many more. At this stage the story was vague and the investigations were not yet completed. Ironically, as significant as this letter was in sparking my interest in learning more about this voyage, it was deemed worthy for only minimal use as a primary source in the book. This is an example of how a story from the past can blossom from the tiniest seed.

While the story of the 1817 voyage of the *Chapman* as told in this book is not limited by any archival rules restricting access to sources, there are some limitations. Some material simply does not survive and certain individuals have remained stubbornly elusive. What I have attempted to capture insofar as the available sources allow, is the first-hand point-of-view of life on board a convict ship. The perspectives are mixed. Sometimes we hear from inside the prison on the ship and at other times we hear from the senior command structure of the voyage. The story tries to illustrate the ordinary lived experience from multiple viewpoints and does not just focus on the dramatic and salacious moments of the journey.

This book is not intended as an in-depth academic examination of a convict voyage or the transportation system as a whole. Such analysis is purposely limited in favour of telling a story. To provide the broadest possible context the book is developed across three stages, opening with the best available accounts of the months before the ship departed on the journey. Once the voyage begins the reader will join the crew as they make a routine stop at the port of St Jago in the Cape Verde islands. The purpose of including moments like this is to weave the full tapestry of the convict voyage. The final section of the book deals with the aftermath of the voyage. What were the consequences? What became of the main players? What became of the system? The function of illustrating the 'before and after' histories of the voyage is to demonstrate that it did not happen in isolation. This is a story of brutality and killing that did not begin with the departure from one port and embarkation at another. As well as recalling the horrors that unfolded during the sailing, the book offers some insight into the world of the ordinary criminal. The stories, profiles and anecdotes that permeate the book are intended to continue to broaden our understanding of the criminal poor in early nineteenth-century Ireland.

Introduction

During the eighteenth and nineteenth centuries the ritual of convict transportation became a fully embedded component of the structure of penal discipline in Ireland. Men and women who were deemed to have contravened the norms of society by breaking the law were legally expelled from their home country for periods of seven or fourteen years, or life, the sentence depending upon the severity of their deviant act. The pattern was familiar. The police, or those configurations that preceded their creation, detected a criminal act. The accused was brought before a magistrate and questioned. He or she had almost certainly emerged from the impoverished and low-income classes. They were subjected to a trial where, if they were found guilty, a sentence was passed. A sentence of transportation was the common fate for what by modern standards would be seemingly innocuous crimes. From stealing animals to passing forged currency, from picking pockets to basic theft, the likelihood of exile to the newly colonised territory of New South Wales on the eastern side of what would later become Australia, became a real possibility for the average Irish petty criminal.

Shiploads of men and women were discarded from Irish society, beginning with the departure of the first convict transportation ship from the country in 1791. The overwhelming majority of those voyages departed from the Cove of Cork, known today as the town of Cobh, adjacent to modern-day Cork city in the south of Ireland. Designed to punish, eliminate and deter criminality from ordinary life, the reality of transportation brought with it a whole range of new social problems and many of those unfolded on the journey to the other side of the world. This book will explore the way in which many of those problems were played out on one voyage that departed from the Cove of Cork in March 1817. During the four-month voyage of the *Chapman*, the convicts, sailors, soldiers and officers variously experienced prolonged light-deprived incarceration, starvation, torture, suspicion, a real or perceived threat of mutiny, and death by gunfire. The story of the voyage and its aftermath will be told using the words of those who were there. Although their versions were often conflicting, the voices of convict witnesses, officers and sailors are worth hearing for the sense of despair and fear that is conveyed from what became a blood-soaked voyage.

The book attempts to accurately record the story of the voyage at all possible stages. The real story of such journeys usually begins before the ship even sets sail and so we first encounter the *Chapman* as it leaves the naval dockyard at Deptford on the Thames. After many weeks of preparation in Cork we begin the journey proper, crossing some of the great waterways of the world, stopping for refreshment and resupplying at the exotic port of Porto Praya, before continuing alongside the mysterious continent of Africa, around the Cape of Good Hope and onwards towards the east side of the land mass that would become known as Australia. After the voyage is over we will examine the aftermath. Insofar as is possible, we will try to determine what became of the main players. Did the voyage have an impact on the transportation process? How, if at all, did any of the *Chapman* convicts make their mark on their new homeland? How did the system progress in the Cove of Cork long after the *Chapman* was just a footnote in popular memory?

The Transportation System

To describe the practice of convict transportation as a means to an end in ridding a given jurisdiction of its more deviant inhabitants would be to simplify a phenomenon that was somewhat more complex in its origins.

Emsley considers exile in the early modern period where the forced removal of an individual from a city state was seen as a considerable punishment. He cites the example of Russia, where penance was achieved through flogging but redemption would mean banishment. There was some permanence to this, however, because in the Russian context, banishment was used as a way of populating Siberia.[1] In Britain – and by extension Ireland – transportation as an alternative form of penal discipline and punishment had its origins in the seventeenth century. It was enshrined in legislation in the Transportation Act in 1718.[2] Until the 1770s this meant that Britain's convicts were despatched to the American colonies but following the War of Independence this avenue was closed. With the 'discovery' of Australia for Britain in 1776 came the opportunity for new colonial adventures and a so-called dumping-ground for criminals. Between 1788 and 1868 a total of 825 transportation ships carried in excess of 167,000 convicted criminals from England and Ireland to Australia.[3] Scholars appear somewhat divided on the overall numbers transported. For example, Hirst argues that 187,000 were exiled in this way, the majority after 1815.[4] Most agree that the system peaked in the 1830s with around 5,000 individuals transported each year. During the seventy-seven-year period from 1791 to 1868 some 37,432 Irish men and women were transported to the colonies of New South Wales, Van Diemen's Land and Western Australia.[5] Irish-born convicts arrived in Australia from the very beginning due to the fact that an estimated 4 per cent of those convicted in Britain originate from Ireland.

The first prisoners taken directly from Ireland left the southern port of Cobh on board the *Queen* in 1791 with 155 convict passengers and four of their children.[6] It is believed that over 1,300 convicts were transported from places other than Great Britain or Ireland, including India, Canada, the Cape of Good Hope, Bermuda and Mauritius, among others. O'Toole suggests that many of these were soldiers transported for mutiny, desertion or other military-related offences.[7] Morgan defines transportation as a 'halfway house between sentencing to hanging and recommendations for whipping and branding'.[8] Indeed the somewhat patchy records for capital punishment in nineteenth-century Ireland show a growing reliance on the option to commute a sentence of hanging to one of transportation.

Transportation from Ireland

When a sentence of transportation was handed down, a convict was typically sent back to the nearest local or county gaol until the authorities
were ready to put the process in motion. Those to be transported from
the southern Irish counties awaited their fate inside the city gaol in Cork.
In 1817 a convict depot or type of holding prison was established in
Cork to provide interim accommodation for the increasing numbers
awaiting transportation.[9] A government investigation into alleged financial abuses within the prison system in Cork was published just eleven
days prior to the departure of the *Chapman* in March 1817 and provides
a useful window into the pre-transportation experience. Specifically,
the commissioners were appointed to look into the prison in Cork city
and any transportation ships awaiting departure in Cork harbour. The
inquiry began with the convict ships because any delay caused by an
awaited investigation might cause a financial burden to the transportation
voyage. The investigators considered it would be judicious not to examine the convicts under oath as with close investigation the truth could
be obtained without resorting to the usual formality.[10] The resulting
testimony confirms much about the somewhat chaotic early nineteenth-
century prison as it reveals about the pre-transportation process.[11] The
detail provided in the report provides much of the backdrop for chapter
one of the book. While the *Chapman* prepared to set sail, the convicts
must surely have been pondering their future in a land far removed from
anything they could possibly imagine.

The Composition of New South Wales

Prior to the arrival of Captain Cook in 1776 it is widely accepted that
human beings lived in and around the colony that would be called New
South Wales for some 40,000 years. The society encountered by Cook
and later the First Fleet in 1788 was essentially hunter-gatherer in nature:
the first proper European settlement was not the beginning of Australian
history, it was merely the beginning of modernisation. By the begin-

ning of the second decade of the nineteenth century the known districts of New South Wales were growing in population and sophistication. In 1810 Sydney had 6,158 inhabitants. Paramatta was home to 1,807, Hawkesbury to 2,389 and Newcastle to 100 people. This brought a total of 10,454 residents, 2,220 of whom were women, 5,513 were men and 2,721 children. It was estimated that a quarter to a third of the population was convict. The 1810 count also included data on Port Dalrymple and Hobart's Town in Van Diemen's Land, which was south of Sydney and was home to some 1,321 people. An additional 177 people lived at Norfolk Island.[12] The inhabited portion of the land mass that came to be known as Australia was tiny by comparison to what it would be during the following century.

New South Wales was bordered to the north, west and south by the Blue Mountains and in 1810 the land beyond that range had not yet been explored by the settlers. Official accounts stated that the farthest distance travelled thus far was about 100 miles but only the first 60 could be described as suitable for agriculture. About half the land in the settled territory was believed to be barren, with 21,000 acres in cultivation and 74,000 in pasture. A government census of livestock shows an impressive supply of animals. There were over 1,000 horses, 193 bulls, 6,351 cows, 4,732 oxen, 33,818 sheep, 1,732 goats and 8,992 hogs.[13] A small percentage of these were held by the government and converted to meat for the public supply. Apart from natural crop failures and other incidental interventions it appears that the colony was self-sufficient in most ways.

The journey between Europe and New South Wales was fraught with many dangers and challenges, not least of which was the threat of mutiny against a cold-blooded or cruel captain and his officers.

Mutiny at Sea

Adams points out that the conditions under which sailors and prisoners served, worked and lived on convict voyages between 1787 and the final such sailing in 1868 fed into the unceasing rumours of mutinies by both cohorts of passenger.[14] The subject of convict mutiny on the voyage to

Australia has not been widely explored by historians for the reason that only one vessel is known to have been successfully seized in this way during the transportation period. The *Lady Shore* was a female convict vessel that left the port of Falmouth in England on 8 June 1797 bound for Port Jackson, New South Wales. According to an account by one of the officers, John Black, who remained loyal to the captain, the mutiny began at about a quarter past four in the morning of 1 August when the chief mate, named Lambert, entered his cabin. Black grabbed his pistol and fired but only managed to shoot the hat off the head of one of the mutineers.[15] In this case it was not the convicts but the guards, a detachment from the New South Wales Corps who, according to Hughes, rose up in the name of the French Republic. After a relatively bloodless takeover of the ship they sailed to Montevideo, where they were accepted as political refugees. They handed over the female prisoners to Spanish colonial 'ladies of quality'.[16] The takeover was executed by twenty-two of the soldiers and crew, nine of whom were previously French prisoners of war. The female convicts later described how the plot was 'carefully timed' and well carried out. Maxwell-Stewart argues that the voyage of the *Lady Shore* was 'hardly typical' but in fact revealed the thin line between convict, soldier and sailor. It was believed that the female convicts below deck were not 'innocent bystanders' but were involved sexually with the soldiers and crew. This theory claims that when attempts were made to discontinue this interaction the mutiny was the outcome.[17]

The opportunity to pre-plan a mutiny was something that was to be expected for two reasons. The majority of those on board were there against their will and existed in poor and often unsanitary conditions on their way to a place of exile. Secondly, it is likely that in the months prior to the voyage the convicts were holed up either in a hulk, in the case of England, or a prison, in the case of Ireland. In such circumstances the combination of apprehension and resentment could easily give way to conspiracy and plotting. This appears to be the situation in the case of the vessel the *Argyle*. Significantly, it emerged later that the ship's surgeon, Henry Brock, was tipped off about a possible plot to seize the vessel before the voyage commenced. While the ringleader of the plotters did not set sail, five of his conspirators did and so Brock took the initiative of distributing them across the ship and out of physical proximity with each other, to lessen the opportunity for conspiracy. In fact, the conspirators had previously been incarcerated on the *Captivity* hulk, where the plot was allegedly hatched.[18] This was one of the central accusations against the alleged mutineers on board the *Chapman*, which will be examined later.

Citing Bateson, Adams points out that compared with shipwreck and disease, the number of those injured or killed in mutinies was small but the number of riots and other disturbances was probably greater than what was reported. It was not in the interest of a ship's master to report every incident or suspected attempt to overtake a ship because it would reflect poorly on him and his officers. He noted that the mutiny with the highest number of fatalities appears to have been on another ship departed from Cork. The *Hercules* left Ireland on 29 November 1801 with fourteen rioting prisoners killed exactly one month later.[19]

The Chapman

The *Chapman* was built at Whitby dockyard in 1777 and consisted of two decks. The vessel was just over 119 ft long with a keel of over 95 ft. The principal managing owner of the ship was Abel Chapman and the maiden voyage appears to have taken place in 1780–81.[20] Now in service to the East India Company, that first journey took the vessel to Madras and Bengal. From then until 1817 it toured the world visiting such diverse locations as China, North America and the Cape of Good Hope. Rebuilt in 1811 and refurbished in 1815 the next phase of life would be altogether different for the *Chapman*.[21] Around 1815 the ship appears to have been decommissioned for use as a military support vessel before being hired out to the Royal Navy for the purposes of convict transportation. Not originally constructed for this purpose, it would be a further two years before the experienced ship set sail for New South Wales, albeit guided by very inexperienced hands.

A note on the sources

The story of the 1817 voyage of the *Chapman* as told in this book is revealed where possible through the words of those who made the journey. To that end it is worth repeating that the people on the ship had differing perspectives on the course of the many events that marked those four months. The captain of the ship and his senior officers were all professional seaman. They were not professional gaolers. Every time a transportation ship set sail to New South Wales, these two professional worlds collided. The mediator between the gaoler and the gaoled was usually a small military detachment. The viewpoints that tell the story of this voyage, therefore, are sometimes fundamentally different. Where possible, the common threads have been identified and put forward as agreed facts. Elsewhere, where the facts around some event or controversy were contested, this is put forward as a perspective.

The central set of sources that drives our knowledge of the *Chapman* episode comes in the form of documents held within a volume of correspondence known as the Historical Records of Australia. These items were copied by the governing authorities in New South Wales and sent to London at regular intervals, presumably to provide accountability on the administration of the colony. Among the packages returned to London were the daily logs or journals of the captain of the ship and his surgeon-superintendent. These were seized by the authorities when problems were identified at the end of the journey in Sydney. They give only a 'bare-bones' account of the day-to-day events on the ship and investigators noted key omissions such as the lack of a reference to a shooting incident on the *Chapman* around 17 April 1817. When added to other documents in the volume including lines of correspondence between the ship commander and officers, as well as with government officials, they do assist in forming a context for some of the more dramatic events of the voyage.

As the story unfolds it will become obvious that much of the narrative is drawn from the different investigations that took place during the months of September and October 1817. During these weeks, many of the significant actors in the drama were questioned at length by investigators. From a command point of view, this included all of the senior officers including the captain, surgeon-superintendent, three mates, military leaders, several soldiers and a number of regular sailors. On the prisoner side was lengthy testimony from multiple convict witnesses, some of whom were believed to be alleged conspirators and others who were known to have witnessed certain occurrences with their own eyes.

While these accounts would be expected to offer not only differing perspectives and contradictory intelligence, closer inspection finds that there are many points of agreement. For the historian and the reader of these documents it is essential to remember that an awareness of perspective is fundamental to the most accurate interpretation of the material. The concluding chapter of the book will summarise and address the most disputed questions still outstanding at the end of the voyage and the subsequent legal investigations.

We come to know the 200 men transported on the *Chapman* far better than we would if they had remained at home within the prison system of Ireland. This comes through a process of familiarisation and is not unique to every individual, nor is it exhaustive. Our first encounter with the convicts is through the standard list of names that was generated at the time the ship left port in Cork. This document recorded data such as name, age, place of birth, place of trial and ultimate fate. For this voyage, the latter was only noted if the person died at sea. The next encounter with the transported men happens usually by working backwards in time to the register of inmates for the Irish-based prison in the jurisdiction where their offence was committed and prosecuted. Prison registers prove an effective window into a sizeable and vibrant element of society in nineteenth-century Ireland. As well as the details provided in the transportation list, we have some additional data on the convicts such as physical features, religion, next of kin and criminal act. With a profile of each man gradually forming, the next logical step is to trace his criminal act through contemporary newspapers in an effort to find reporting on his trial. This line of enquiry has only moderate success. Not every stolen beast was the subject of a lengthy court proceeding and subsequent newspaper report. Not every forged note was deemed worthy of inclusion in the national press. When the criminal adventures of these low-level deviants were reported, however, it tended to be in great detail. Not only do we learn about the wicked exploits of the thief or the vandal but we peek through a window into the world of the ordinary Irish poor, urban and rural. We learn something about a way of life, a struggle for existence, a journey along that fine line between right and wrong. These are the *Chapman* convicts whose stories can be told in the greatest detail.

The appendices to this book will present some 'bare bones' data on the fate of the convicts who were fortunate enough to survive the voyage in 1817. The criminal classes banished to New South Wales from Ireland and England experienced different fates once their sentences expired. They generally passed through a set procedure that included the possibility of a conditional or absolute pardon, a ticket of leave or a land grant. Built into all of this was the option to return home or indeed to bring family members to the colony from Europe. Where the records survive, the names of *Chapman* convicts who availed of pardons, land grants and an eventual certificate of freedom, are included in the appendices. It must be stated at the outset that while these records are far from complete they do provide something of an insight into the general fate of the convicts, all of whom were witnesses to horror on the high seas en route from Cork to Port Jackson. Including these incomplete records in the appendices is intended to demonstrate some level of continuity to a post-voyage existence.

1

The Countdown to Chaos

In March 1817 a convict transportation ship left the Cove of Cork bound for New South Wales. As it left the port that is known today as Cobh there was little to set the *Chapman* apart from the many other vessels that transported the disgraced and the sinful to their exile in Australia. On board were 200 male convicts, thirty-two soldiers of the 46th Regiment and a crew of forty men under the leadership of the allegedly drunken and incompetent Captain Drake. Yet when the ship anchored in Sydney Cove on 27 July 1817, it laid bare the story of a nightmarish four-month voyage that was marred by unrelenting horror, torture, starvation, death, and tales of a mutiny that never happened. Convict transports had long been known as 'hell-ships' but this voyage was different. When the doors were opened at the end of the journey, 160 gaunt and emaciated men emerged from the prison below deck where they were dazed and blinded by the sunlight of a strange new world. Of the original convict cargo, twelve died in violent circumstances at the hands of the soldiers. Close to thirty lay wounded in the ship's hospital. While the surviving convicts and the crew told conflicting stories of their voyage, all of the accounts had certain features in common. The storm that consumed the journey of the *Chapman* from Cork to Sydney was not one brought about by nature but by a climate of fear, degradation, intrigue and misplaced vengeance. For the government officials who routinely inspected arriving convict transports in

Sydney, the bloodstained decks of the *Chapman* summoned up terrifying images of a voyage that went horribly wrong.

The Guardian of the Night – Dublin, June 1816

In the newspapers and in the courtrooms they were known as the Guardians of the Night. For decades the men of the parish watch were a key line of defence for the citizens of Dublin against the invisible forces that threatened them during the hours of darkness. In early June 1816, sometime between the hours of one and two in the morning, the watchman doing his nightly round on Bishop Street stopped in his tracks. Despite the late hour, the elderly Ferdinand Mervin was accustomed to noticing anything out of place. His eyes were trained to the darkness and at this moment they were fixed on the suspicious looking fellow outside the home of the tallow-chandler Ann Butler. Mervin approached the man, who was carrying a bundle in his hand. 'What are you up to at this hour of the morning?' It was a reasonable question from a watchman whose duty it was to patrol the streets in the days when professional policing was still a work in progress. Before his quarry had an opportunity to respond, Mervin noticed two violins and a hat lying on the ground near the man's feet. At this moment several other watchmen appeared and together they apprehended the man, whose name was Peter Allen. They took him to the nearest watch-house.

Along with Robert Gilbert, the constable on duty that night, some of the watchmen headed back towards Mrs Butler's house, where they found another suspicious character, John Ennis. He too was conveyed to the watch-house and upon 'questioning' he confessed to having robbed Mrs Butler's and passed on the spoils of his exploits to a number of accomplices. Acting on information from Ennis, the constable and his watchmen hurried to a house on nearby Kevin Street, where they encountered a man coming out the front door. Instantly reversing course, the man rushed upstairs and onto the roof of the house, where his journey was halted by Constable Gilbert. In the room from which the man entered the roof the officers discovered a woman, who was in the process of concealing various objects under the straw of her bed. A search of the space uncovered nine shirts, a brown greatcoat, four hams, a piece of bacon, the pattern of a new muslin gown, some portions of new linen, a grey cloak and a blanket, among other items.

Back at the watch-house the man apprehended on the roof named himself as Michael Kennedy and the woman identified herself as Mary Neill. By the early hours of the morning Mrs Butler, the owner of the house on Bishop Street, was at the watch-house; where she identified some of the stolen items found in the possession of Peter Allen, the man first spotted by Watchman Mervin. Items not belonging to Mrs Butler personally were claimed by her lodgers. It was later observed that the thieves were only beginning the robbery on Mrs Butler's house when they were interrupted by the watchmen. Indeed, hers was not likely to be the only house they targeted that night.[22]

Peter Allen, who was apprehended whilst standing guard during the break-in, was sentenced to seven years' transportation. John Ennis, who was caught red-handed inside the house, was sentenced to death. This was later commuted to transportation.[23] Anyone who doubted the potential of the watchman only needs to look at the fate of Allen and Ennis. Neither vigilante nor professional policeman, the watchman was an early version of the constable on his beat. His power was limited but his reach was far. The parish watch had a reputation for being ineffective and this was probably well-founded. The actions of the aging Ferdinand Mervin, however, proved that there were exceptions. He had a keen eye and good local knowledge. His decisive action resulted in a pair of low-level petty burglars finding themselves at the centre of a ghastly four-month nightmare that played out across oceans and seas on both hemispheres of the earth. Their minds would be forever stained with the blood of a dozen murdered cell-mates. The stench of a floating prison whose doors never opened would haunt their senses. The journey would have enormous implications for a colonial government and its masters at the heart of the British Empire. They were only a part of that journey because they decided to break into the home of Ann Butler. Was it carefully planned in advance or another sudden impulse of the petty criminal classes? They were only there because the watchman noticed something out of place on a dark night on Bishop Street.

Six months later

The fateful journey from Cork to New South Wales began not in Ireland but on the River Thames in London. Before leaving for Australia it was typical for transportation vessels to undergo preparation at one of the royal dockyards of the British Navy. The *Chapman* was anchored at the dockyard at Deptford, which had become known as the 'cradle of the Navy' due to its importance to exploration and the empire since it was founded in 1513 by Henry VIII. Deptford dockyard was somewhat of a crossroads of the world. The facility comprised a sprawling array of docks, warehouses and workshops, all necessary to maintain the fleet of a successful seafaring nation. The dockyard workers not only carried out any essential repairs to the ships but also re-fitted them with necessary equipment such as cables, sails or bedding. Alongside the dockyard was a victualling yard, itself a type of dock where the many ships that passed through Deptford were supplied with all manner of necessities including dry food and meat, alcohol and bread. On 11 December 1816 the *Chapman* left behind the noise and the energy of the dockyard to begin the first part of an epic journey to the Australian colonies. The first destination and the official starting point of the voyage was the Cove of Cork.

One month later

The *Chapman* arrived at Cork on Thursday, 9 January 1817 where further and final preparations got under way for the transportation voyage. Although not as lavish or cosmopolitan as Deptford, Cove was probably more significant to the voyage as it was the official launching-point. Around the same time, a vessel named the *Atlas* arrived from Dublin bearing a party of convicts that would be transported on board the *Chapman*. During the following weeks, while both ships were docked alongside each other, the surgeon-superintendent of the *Chapman*, Alexander Dewar, and the master (or captain) of the *Atlas* became acquainted. The captain managed to convince the surgeon that the convicts that he had just conveyed from Dublin were notorious and violent characters who attempted to take over the *Atlas* on the voyage to Cork. The allegations are difficult to prove or disprove but seem to have been enough to sow seeds of fear and mistrust among the senior command of the *Chapman*, setting them on a high-stakes collision course that was played out during the months ahead.

The process of preparing for the convict voyage was not as straightforward as loading the human cargo on board and setting sail. Despite some initial work in Deptford, fittings were in need of repair. Supplies were in need of replenishing. The crew and military guard would need to be properly assembled and deemed fit for the gruelling four-month voyage to Sydney.

The Cove of Cork

Towards the end of the eighteenth century, the harbour of Cork, known as Cove, was described as 'the largest and best secured in the kingdom where ships of any size and number may ride in perfect safety'.[24] Writing in 1834, the English travel writer Henry Inglis described the Cove of Cork as a 'considerable town, and a pretty town' about 9 miles by road and 11 miles by water, from the city of Cork.[25] To English people, the Cove of Cork suggested 'a large sea basin' close to Cork but in the region itself it was known as 'the harbour'. The word 'Cove' was assigned to the town that emerged in that harbour or sea basin.[26]

An 1817 government investigation into the world of convict detention in Cork reveals a curious array of bureaucrats and functionaries drawn together in a complex financial web where each one was concerned with their own portion of the 'per prisoner' allocation provided by the Treasury. The extent to which each individual personally profited from these transactions was not answered by the investigators but there is clearly some room for interpretation in certain cases. One of the processes that a convict ship underwent in advance of the voyage was that of victualing. Richard Sainthill was the Victualling Agent for the convict deport in Cork. This individual was appointed by the Victualling Board, whose overall remit was to ensure that ships and vessels of the British Navy, army and related organisations – as well as those on board – were stocked with sufficient food and drink for the course of their journey. In the administration of their duties the board and its agents demonstrated varying levels of competence.[27]

Captain Sainthill outlined how his written instructions from the Chief Secretary were 'to provide for a certain number of months for the convicts for the voyage, and a certain quantity is to be laid in to give up to the colony'. He was also required to provide fresh beef while they were incarcerated on the vessels prior to leaving Cork Harbour.[28] Sainthill was unique among those examined for the investigation as he only visited the gaol in Cork once in his twenty-year career in the city. His relevance to the 1817 investigation was that his office was part of a network of financial transactions that involved the convicts on the transportation vessels. A medical storekeeper at the victualing yard at Deptford would have already supplied the surgeon with all his equipment, medicines and instruments for the voyage.[29]

Waiting in hell-on-earth

In the immediate period before they boarded their transportation ship many of the convicts were held within the prison system in Cork. Those from Dublin arrived on the *Atlas*. The city gaol was described in harrowing terms. The government officials that happened to be carrying out an investigation in the city at the time essentially described a vision of hell-on-earth that was overcrowded with prisoners, including many awaiting embarkation. One man lay dying on the ground with inflammation of the lungs. There was no yard and neither was there a space for prisoners to take in fresh air. Even the toilets – or privies – were indoors and very exposed.[30]

During 1817 the gaoler or keeper of the prison was John Welsh. In evidence to the investigators he claimed that the physical security of the facility was deeply flawed. He described how, at one end of the complex there was only a single brick wall separating it from the next building. Welsh described how he found it necessary to pay 'secret-service money' to certain prisoners in order to gather information on potential escape plots. He claimed that both the sheriff and the grand jury were well aware of the shortcomings in the building and had failed to provide any resources or plan by way of improvement. Indeed, the grand jury sent a committee to inspect the premises during every assizes session but nothing changed. Welsh argued to his interrogators that short of knocking down and rebuilding the gaol entirely, there was nothing structural that could be done to improve security. His problem, in the eyes of the investigators, was his employment of assistant-gaoler Thomas Harding for three years as a human response to a problem that may have had a structural solution. John Welsh and Thomas Harding were brothers-in-law.[31]

Criminal prisoners in Cork *county* gaol enjoyed a diet consisting of 8lb 11oz of bread, 24lb of potatoes and twenty-one pints of milk per week. They were not provided with a monetary allowance but shirts were made available by the county and expenses for other clothing needs were sometimes met by the grand juries. Unlike the later prisons, the authorities did not have the power to force the convicts into labour. The gaoler employed the debtor prisoners, who had no gaol allowance, in pumping water for the prison as well as sweeping and cleaning. They were paid with an allowance of provisions equivalent to the cost of hiring a labourer on the outside. Female prisoners were employed in what were gender-appropriate occupations for that time. These included washing the bedding and shirts as well as making clothing. For this they earned sixpence per day. Whether the debtors or the female prisoners were always fully recompensed for their labours is an unresolved question and was sometimes a source of controversy at official level.

The ship becomes a prison

From the moment of the arrival in Cove, the decks of the *Chapman* were a hive of activity. Before the convicts were boarded onto the ship it was the duty of the local prison doctor to examine the vessel and declare it fit for human habitation. Dr Robert Harding was the Medical Officer for the local prison and convict transportation system established in Cork and he had the power to prevent a vessel from departing from the port if he found that any of the convicts or crew were unfit to travel. He was a land-bound official and, unlike the surgeon-superintendent, he would not accompany the ship on the onward journey.

When the *Chapman* arrived in Cork, Dr Harding decided it was not fit to receive convicts. A reconstruction operation was undertaken to move the hospital section from the front to the back of the ship and certain other repairs were carried out to make the vessel 'convict-ready'. No

convicts were boarded while workmen were carrying out these altera-
tions as practice had always dictated that the mix of sharp implements
and convicted criminals was not a good idea. Dr Harding stated that he
would 'keep them as short a time as possible on board previous to their
sailing, in order that the ship may be kept clean and better aired'. As it
happened, there were not yet enough convicts present in the gaols or
ships of Cork to fill the *Chapman*.

Preparation for the voyage continued apace during the month of
January. Some unrest was identified among the crew with the discharge
of thirteen men for different reasons, most notably dissatisfaction with
what they felt was a slave-like existence on the ship. The life of a seaman
was not an enviable one and his terms of employment usually meant that
he was not paid until the end of the voyage. The occurrence of these
discharges during the first week or more after arrival in Cork is likely
indicative of a difficult December voyage from London, which perhaps
challenged either the stamina or the commitment of the men for the
months-long journey ahead.

At the end of January the ship began taking on board some of the
equipment and food that would be needed for the convicts. These
included everything from padlocks to bread, clothing to hats and beds.
The carpentry work was completed on 2 February and the prison section was deemed ready to received convicts. The supply of necessary
materials was accelerated with the arrival of stocks of beds, clothing,
irons, rivets, hammers, chisels, punches and an anvil. On 5 February the
Chapman received the first consignment of convicts with the arrival of
thirty-four men. Between then and 11 February the entire remaining
convict capacity was embarked but the ship would not begin its journey for another month.[32] To alleviate the boredom and take care of the
duties necessary to keep life on the ship running smoothly, some of the
prisoners were allocated certain roles. Three men were appointed cooks
while two others were assigned to fill the cisterns and handle the swabs.
As well as this the crew began to allow twelve convicts at a time up on
deck for one hour. This was important both while docked and at sea
because it relieved the boredom and tension in the dungeon that was
the ships' prison. Judicial investigators later found that the decision to
allow only twelve men at a time up on deck arose either from 'exces-

sive natural timidity or cruelty in the Superintendent'.[33] None of this was enough to avoid unrest on the vessel, however, with some minor infractions among the convicts and indeed the crew. Two convicts were handcuffed for fighting while another man, possibly a crew member, for an unstated offence.

As the departure date approached, the ship was supplied with some of the more necessary stocks that would sustain it until its first port of call. These included clothing, water kegs, porringers, towels, soap, tobacco, vinegar and iron hoops. The convicts were divided into 'messes' of twelve men and each group slept and ate together, with certain individuals being delegated tasks such as food distribution or cleaning. Messes were also 'mustered' or marched together in groups above deck for inspection purposes or to take in fresh air. This was a well-rehearsed means of keeping some sort of order on the ship once the journey got under way. Organising the prisoners in this way was also part of the growing momentum toward the beginning of their voyage and exile. The overall responsibility for maintaining order fell to a number of key individuals.

The official responsibilities of Captain Drake

The captain or commander of the *Chapman* for this voyage to New South Wales was John Drake. Prior to the *Chapman* departing the River Thames in December 1816 and her voyage to Cork, Captain Drake received a standard but specific set of duties or instructions from the Transport Commissioners. These were essentially his rules of conduct for the voyage and are significant because by the end of July 1817 he had violated most of them. The first instruction addressed what was probably the most significant relationship between any senior officials on one of these transports, the one between the master or captain and the surgeon-superintendent. Drake was formally notified that Alexander Dewar was appointed to that role and as such his wishes in the area of the management and treatment of the convicts must be fully respected and carried out. Although this was a formal notification, the reality was that the men had a close relationship and cooperated with apparent ease throughout the voyage, often to the detriment of the convicts.

The second area of concern was the general well-being of the convicts. Drake was instructed to equip the ship with everything necessary 'for keeping her clean and sweet, the better to preserve the health of the Convicts and Passengers during their voyage to New South Wales'.[34] As well as this the captain and surgeon were ordered to allow a number of convicts up on deck to take in fresh air on every day that the weather allowed. While the number was not specified it can be assumed that the intention was to operate a rota system whereby every individual had an opportunity to leave the prison quarters at routine intervals. Additionally, the convict 'berths' were to be properly cleaned and ventilated on a regular basis. It was ordered that all of these actions were noted in a logbook as and when they happened. His own log entries would later prove that Drake disregarded the well-being of his convicts on a permanent basis from the second month of the voyage onwards.

If the *Chapman* docked at the Cape of Good Hope on the journey to New South Wales the captain was ordered to take on board any number of convicts for which he had accommodation and was desired by the governor there. Upon eventual return to London he was required to produce a certificate that included a declaration of satisfaction by the governor and other officials in New South Wales. This document particularly referred to the 'victualing and treatment of the convicts on the voyage'. If he demonstrated 'assiduity and humanity' then he would be rewarded with a gift at the discretion of the Secretary of State. If there was evidence of neglect or under-performance in these essential duties then he would be 'prosecuted with the utmost severity'.[35] The extent to which any of these instructions were mere token gestures to satisfy the concerns of penal reformers and other observers would later be tested to a degree not seen on any other voyage during the convict transportation era.

The all-powerful Superintendent-Surgeon Dewar

Transportation ships had long been places of hardship and danger for the unfortunate convicts, who were reluctant and court-ordered travellers. Such was the level of degradation and danger on board that the loss of life approached scandalous levels, culminating in fifty-four deaths on board the *Surrey* in 1814. As well as convicts, the fatalities included the master, both mates and the surgeon; all were lost to typhus. Two other vessels, *General Hewitt* and the *Three Bees*, also suffered heavy losses and attracted official attention. Once the disaster was discovered in Sydney, an Assistant Colonial Surgeon, William Redfern, was appointed to investigate and make recommendations. Not only did his report become what has been described as one of Australia's most significant contributions to public health, it also marked the beginning of a new and somewhat safer phase of the transportation era.

As well as suggesting more generous allowances of wine and lemon juice to fend off scurvy, he also recommended better clothing and washing. Central to his proposal was an enhanced role for the surgeon, who should be able to confront any brutal or incompetent practices by a potentially drunken captain.[36] Redfern demanded that the surgeon be properly qualified and experienced, and should not hold a 'subordinate state of authority in relation to the master of the ship'.[37] His recommendations were largely taken on board. From 1815, the surgeon-superintendent was a permanent and powerful fixture on all convict voyages to Australia. All holders of this office were chosen from within the Royal Navy and essentially they were charged with control of the convicts.[38] Using the experience of the *Surrey* disaster, the authorities devised a new and more progressive regime where this office-holder would bear huge responsibility for ensuring not only the health but the survival of the convicts.

Serving in the Royal Navy since 1802, Alexander Dewar was appointed the surgeon-superintendent of the *Chapman* for this voyage and on 28 November 1816 he too received a set of instructions from the Transport Commissioners in London. The recommendations of William Redfern are plain to see. Again, the relationship with the captain was front and centre of his responsibility, with the clearly stated order that his remit only extended to the care and management of the convicts and not the navigation of the ship. Any departure from his guidelines towards treatment of the convicts must be fully logged and explained in a journal to be made available to the governor of New South Wales upon arrival in Sydney. It was also his duty to ensure that no unauthorised supplies or other material be brought on board the vessel upon departure or at any port at which it may land on the voyage.

Dewar was presented with a number of clear instructions in the area of feeding the convicts. The crew and passengers were to receive their allocated rations at all times without variation or deduction.[39] The commissioners appear to have provided Dewar with some latitude here, however, as the instruction specified that 'crew and passengers' should be given the allocation without exception, but does not state if 'passengers' includes the convicts in this instance. Everything was to be properly cooked and distributed at the correct mealtime, again without deviation. Any meat purchased for the convicts and passengers during the voyage must be 'good and wholesome' and up to Victualing Board standards. He was also instructed in the use of the six-month supply of lemon juice and sugar that would be placed on board the ship before departure. A half ounce each of sugar and lemon juice would be mixed and given to each man daily as a sherbet, or it could be added to the wine allowed to convicts. Distribution of these drinks did not begin until the ship was at sea for between three weeks to a month.

The crucial role of a ship's surgeon was, of course, the care of the sick. He was mandated to visit the sick at least twice a day but preferably more often and to administer medical aid as he saw fit. It was essential that he enquired as to the general management, diet, nursing and care of the sick during these visits. The surgeon was also required to walk among the healthy convicts, passengers and crew on a daily basis for a general inspection, while at the same time identifying any possible health issues, complaints or evidence of fever, flux or scurvy. Only patients whose complaints were infectious should be sent to the hospital while those with lesser conditions that could be treated with dietary regulation and sleep should be kept in their own beds.[40] Like Drake in his log entries, Dewar's own words would later prove that he was wholly negligent in his care of sick and injured convicts.

Those in the ship's hospital would likely have infectious complaints so they should have their clothing removed, their hair cut off and be bathed in a tub if at all possible. If a bath was not possible then face, hands and feet should be washed thoroughly in warm water with soap. The linen clothing belonging to sick passengers should be steeped in cold water before being handled and washed properly. Infected woollen clothing should be 'exposed to the fumes of sulphur' but if this was not possible then it should be exposed in the open air for three days. The sick were to be bathed once a week during the voyage. They would be fed on special provisions such as rice, oatmeal, flour, biscuit, raisins and wine, all of which should be requested from the captain.[41] While it was probably unnecessary to provide such guidance to an experienced doctor, the very presentation of written instructions to this particular crew became an important legal issue once the voyage was investigated afterwards.

Cleanliness and ventilation were raised as significant factors for attention by the surgeon. Cabins should be kept as airy and dry as possible under the circumstances. The utmost cleanliness should prevail in 'peoples' persons', as well as in the hospital where both ventilation and warmth were essential.[42] It might be expected that the prison quarters were included in this guidance but this was not specified, another factor that would become crucial later. To assist the surgeon in his work during the voyage, he was directed to appoint a number of healthy and trustworthy convicts to work as attendants. It was not noted whether these individuals would be rewarded for their endeavours either during or after the journey.

While conditions on board convict transport ships undoubtedly improved due to the implementation of these regulations, it is worth noting that because the surgeon-superintendents were drawn from the Royal Navy this was essentially military medicine. Post-1815 naval doctors had honed their medical skills during the Napoleonic wars but this was 'still a hideously primitive business by modern standards'.[43] The new regulations as suggested by Redfern were heretofore carried out on vessels that were often described as 'hell-ships'. While work practices and living conditions may have improved, not much could be done about the reality that a convict transportation ship was a floating prison with limited scope for internal spatial improvement.

'Two hundred Irish rebels': The convicts of the Chapman

During the pre-voyage period in Cork the commander of the *Atlas* spoke to several officers of the *Chapman*, most notably the surgeon-superintendent, Alexander Dewar. He described the prisoners transported from Dublin as 'a turbulent, desperate, dangerous set of Men' and encouraged excessive vigilance on the journey to New South Wales.[44] Dewar later confirmed that many conversations did take place between himself and the officer of the guard and the master of the *Atlas*. They both alleged on several occasions that the convicts they transported from Dublin to Cove were 'very notorious and riotous characters' who had put in place a plan to take control of the *Atlas* but were discovered and prevented. According to Dewar, the sole disruptive incident that took place while the ship remained docked in Cove was that the convicts attempted to pick the locks of the prison one night.[45]

Of the 200 male prisoners on board the *Chapman*, 102 were tried and convicted in Dublin city or county.[46] With over half of the proposed prisoner population originating from Dublin it explains why Dr Harding was forced to wait before filling the vessel. Just ten of the convicts were tried and convicted in Cork. Cities and counties with a fairly close proximity sent fewer numbers. Galway and Limerick, for example, sent five and three prisoners respectively. The courts in Tipperary sent two while Clare, Waterford and Kerry each sent one. The county of Antrim, including the city of Belfast, sent eight men to the *Chapman* while Armagh sent five. Tyrone was the other main contributor from the northern counties with four prisoners. Counties Louth and Longford sent six and four men respectively, while Wicklow and Meath sent three each.[47] The remaining prisoners were fairly evenly dispersed in low digits from all across the island and this contradicts the previously believed notion that transportation from Cork was largely in the service of the southern counties.

At the end of this voyage the Australian newspapers as well as random British officials described the convicts as 200 Irish rebels. At best this could be described as lazy journalism on the part of the press and at worst it was a fabricated anti-Irish sentiment peddled by British government officials because it fitted a certain narrative about Ireland and resistance to the Union. Whatever the situation, the official records of the voyage, presumably generated by officials in the employ of the government in Cork or Sydney, tell a different story about the *Chapman* convicts.

The majority of men on the ship were convicted of the simple crime of felony. For example, thirteen found themselves transported for the offence of the 'felony of wearing apparel', presumably clothing. Similar crimes included the felony of items such as tobacco, paper, plates, meat, money, towels, food, a saddle, silk, hats, lamps, tea trays and pocketbooks. The stories behind some of the offences suggest that many were indeed crimes of opportunity possibly carried out by professional street corner-boys. Others were doubtless crimes of survival where the perpetrator needed to steal to live, to sustain his family. Despite the reputation of transportees as the dregs of humanity, it was a fact that there were few men convicted of violent offences on the *Chapman*. There was only one convicted murderer and just one man charged under the Insurrection Act. Few if any of the remaining offences seem to have been violent in nature, although this cannot be completely ruled out.

An outstanding feature of the criminal code in early nineteenth-century Ireland was the range of offences for which a person could be executed. This was relaxed in later decades but during 1815–16, when most of these men received their sentences, it remained severe. Twenty-eight men on the *Chapman* were originally given a sentence of death, only to have this commuted to one of transportation. Oliver Wallace was the only one convicted of murder. Animal theft was seen as a particularly egregious offence during this period and men found themselves on this voyage for such crimes involving pigs, cows and sheep. It was the theft of horses, however, that was least tolerated by the criminal justice system. Three men were convicted of horse stealing and all were initially sentenced to death before this was commuted to transportation. Such was the value of the horse to the domestic and agricultural economy that there was no tolerance towards those whose activities would interrupt these sectors of daily life. Added to this was the reality that the ownership of horses was a luxury particularly enjoyed by the elite and ruling classes. Likewise, six *Chapman* convicts were convicted of highway robbery and all of these were sentenced to death before being commuted.

Table 1: Principal offences of Chapman convicts

Felony	58
Stealing	33
House Breaking or Robbery	21
Forged Notes	21
Sheep Stealing	10
Highway Robbery	6
Picking Pockets	6
Cow Stealing	6
Horse Stealing	3
Shop Lifting	3
Pig Stealing	2
Murder	1
Offence Under the Insurrection Act	1

Source: New South Wales and Tasmania, Australia Convict Musters, 1806–1849, www.ancestry.com (accessed on 28 April 2016).[48]

One such highway robbery took place on the evening of 27 November 1816. Sarah Parker was walking along the Summerhill area of Dublin at about seven o'clock. She carried a small bundle in her hand. A man she later identified as Thomas Morgan approached her from behind and attempted to snatch the bundle from her arms. Missing his target, Morgan got in front of his victim and punched her on the body before taking the bundle and running. Parker screamed loudly and a number of individuals rushed to her assistance. One of those men, Alexander Anderson, heard the woman's screams and directed two men coming behind him to intervene. Without losing sight of their target, the men made chase against Morgan, whom they quickly apprehended. The bundle, which contained a velvet dress, was recovered from the twenty-one-year-old man. In a subsequent court proceeding the defending lawyer reminded the judge that Morgan did not actually have any weapon that he intended to use against a potential victim. Nor did he use any offensive language or action, other than pushing her away during the altercation. She described this as a blow to her body. The jury recommended mercy for the man during what was a capital case involving possible execution.[49] The judge obliged and in the spring of 1817, Thomas Morgan found himself on the *Chapman* awaiting transportation to New South Wales.

Two future convict passengers of the *Chapman* found themselves involved in what was a somewhat exceptional sitting of the county assizes in Cork in September 1816. At five o'clock on the evening of Thursday 12 September Mr Justice Mayne passed the death sentence on no fewer than fifteen criminals. Five of the men were sentenced for sheep stealing, two for highway robbery, two for 'waylaying, cutting and maiming' a named individual, and four for a similar separate offence. Cornelius and Denis Hourahan, aged fifteen and twenty respectively, were sentenced for the burglary of the house of the Reverend Dan Crowley.[50] While the Hourahan brothers were ultimately to make the voyage to New South Wales, the fate of the remaining thirteen men in that most bloodthirsty of court sittings is not as clear. All five of those named in the sheep stealing incident appear to have been spared the noose and joined the *Chapman*. At eighty years of age, John Connor was one of those five and was the oldest convict on the voyage.[51]

As we have seen, any notion that those transported at the direction of a magistrate on board a vessel to New South Wales and elsewhere were entirely violent or malevolent has long since been shattered by historians. While the passenger list does not make note of the criminal acts of each man transported on the *Chapman*, a cursory examination throws up plenty of evidence of non-violent offending. James Fox was a twenty-five-year-old labourer from Westmeath when he began his voyage on the ship.[52] In February 1816, Fox appeared at Dublin City Sessions Court, where he was accused of possessing banknotes that he knew to be forged. Tobias Burke, a publican in Thomas Street, testified that the note was given to him by Fox, who offered three different explanations as to how it came into his possession. Following a search at the time, the defendant was not found to be carrying any further such forged currency. After a lengthy and hesitant deliberation, the jury found James Fox guilty and he was subsequently sentenced to fourteen years' transportation.[53] Over a year after this conviction he found himself on the *Chapman* in Cork Harbour awaiting his fate.

The possession of forged banknotes was not uncommon among the *Chapman* convicts. In August 1816, Michael Leonard appeared before one of the Ireland's most feared and high-profile judicial figures, Lord Norbury. At the Meath Assizes he was indicted for possessing forged notes of the Bank of Ireland, knowing them to be forged. Three months earlier, Leonard went into the shop of Hugh Duignan at Trim to purchase linen. He presented a thirty-shilling Bank of Ireland note as payment. As Leonard could not write, the shopkeeper put both of their names on the note. The shopkeeper did not realise he had been passed a forged note but Leonard was being watched by a police constable, Joseph Liscence. The policeman observed the thirty-year-old Leonard and noticed that two of the notes in his possession had the same (presumably serial) numbers. Leonard was taken into custody and onwards to Trim gaol, where he was searched by the Inspector, Reverend Mack Wainright. A further thirteen banknotes were found in Leonard's hat and all had the same serial number. A clerk from the Bank of Ireland testified that all the notes involved in the case were forgeries. Michael Leonard was found guilty and sentenced to be transported for fourteen years.

In June 1816, Thomas Connor, a twenty-two-year-old stone cutter from Dublin, appeared at the Dublin City Sessions Court.[54] The defendant's alleged offence was also non-violent but more opportunistic in nature. On 25 March he was drinking at a house in Francis Street and noticed his 'prosecutor',[55] Grogan, who was somewhat inebriated. Connor offered to 'watch over and protect' Grogan in an apparently humanitarian act. In doing so he took temporary possession of his watch and money – approximately forty shillings – with the understanding that they would be returned the next day. The pair continued drinking but Connor failed to return the money and watch, and subsequently avoided a sobered-up Grogan. After being apprehended, Connor claimed that Grogan was actually stolen from by a woman with whom he had 'picked up' at the end of the drinking session. Connor repeated this allegation in court but Grogan denied involvement with any woman on that occasion. The court found Thomas Connor guilty and the Recorder harshly criticised him for 'his base and treacherous conduct to a man whom he had undertaken to protect'.[56] With a seven-year sentence of transportation, he would join James Fox and Michael Leonard on board the *Chapman*.

All were non-violent criminals who were dealt a punishment of lengthy banishment, a sentence that was, in effect, one of permanent exile.

William Leo was to become one of the most significant figures among the convict population on this voyage. In truth, his horrific journey began on the night of 10 June 1816. A native of county Galway, Leo was twenty-seven years old when he appeared before Dublin City Sessions two weeks later. Along with another man, John McKenna, he was charged with breaking into the coach-house of Mrs Blennerhasset at Belvedere Place in Dublin and stealing a set of harnesses and related horse-and-carriage furniture. A servant of Mrs Blennerhasset, Matthew McCarthy, testified that he last saw all of the stolen items in their proper place when he locked the coach-house door between nine and ten o'clock on the night of 10 June. He was 'alarmed' by the watchman early the next morning. The door was broken open and the coach harness and other items were missing. When Matthew Boylan, the watchman, discovered the robbery he ran to the house and woke Mrs Blennerhasset and her servant before setting out in search of the stolen items. He quickly located McKenna and Leo at the corner of nearby Mountjoy Square. They had the stolen items in their possession but did not surrender easily. Boylan caught McKenna by the throat and told him he deserved to hang for his crime. He then 'put [McKenna] into the care of another watchman' while he pursued and apprehended William Leo. It appears that quite a melee ensued, with Leo and McKenna coming off the worst thanks to several blows to the ribs and legs at the hands of the watchmen. In court, both men were found guilty and sentenced to transportation for seven years.[57] Neither William Leo nor his accusers were to know that he would become one of the most brutalised inmates on the voyage to which he was sentenced.

Another key witness to events on the *Chapman* was twenty-two-year-old John Fagan from Dublin. On 23 September 1815 he and three other men entered the dwelling house and tap room of Thomas and Catherine Tierney in Halston Street in Dublin. The men were drinking porter at the bar in the tap room that night around ten o'clock. At some point, Thomas Tierney noticed three of the men walking from the head of the stairs in a private area of the premises. He subsequently discovered that around £200 worth of notes and coins had been stolen from a locked tea chest in his bedroom. The haul included a large quantity of silver including six-shilling pieces, two and sixpenny and tenpenny pieces, all collected in separate cartridges. There were several £1 notes, a £4 note and three £10 notes. Tierney's wife, Catherine, revealed that not only was the locked tea chest contained inside a larger locked chest, but the bedroom door was also locked. All the locks were broken. Fagan was convicted and sentenced to transportation to New South Wales.

During their early 1817 enquiry into the prison system in Cork, the investigators boarded the *Chapman,* where they interviewed two convicts. The ship was fully boarded with a full complement of convicts and awaiting departure. James Talbot was twenty-nine years old and appeared before the Recorder of Dublin in June 1815, where he was convicted of picking pockets and sentenced to be transported for seven years. Talbot was unable to travel due to ill-health and spent the previous sixteen months incarcerated in Cork.[58] This appears to far exceed the length of time that convicts usually spent awaiting their voyage. Fourteen of the 200 criminals on board were listed as having been convicted during 1815 and one in 1814. Three men had a particularly short wait, having been tried in 1817. The remainder were tried in 1816.[59] In testimony described as 'clear, cool and unembarrassed', Talbot confirmed he received a daily allowance of sixpence, which he would use to purchase his potatoes or the occasional glass of spirits. The potatoes were purchased on his behalf by a woman who was paid to attend to the prisoners by a local inspector. He believed she often defrauded the prisoners during the transactions. The alcohol was purchased from a turnkey named Madders. Transactions of this nature were still present in 1817 and were essentially symptomatic of a still unreformed prison system.

The second man interviewed was Patrick Mahony, convicted of an unspecified offence in Cork city in 1816. He was paid not in money but in the form of three shillings' worth of bread per week. He exchanged this, through the same female messenger, for money or potatoes. His friends sometimes brought him porter but neither porter nor spirits would be permitted by the prison authorities unless they were purchased at Lane's pub next door. The investigators pointed out that 'from the exclusion of other person's porter, it may be inferred that the gaoler was interested in the traffic and sale thereof'. Much of this unscrupulous commercial behaviour on the part of prison officials was long present in the prisons of Ireland and England. Gaolers took advantage of the dire and dull existence of their prisoners and were open to bribery and other forms of illegal behaviour in order to exploit their charges, who longed for some relief.

Of the 200-strong prisoner population on the *Chapman*, twenty-nine were teenaged boys ranging between fifteen and nineteen years. Seventy-seven of the convicts were men in their twenties. Thirty-six were aged between thirty and thirty-nine years. Just sixteen men were in their forties and five were in their fifties. One prisoner was sixty years old. The oldest was the previously mentioned John Connor from Bantry in Cork who, at the age of eighty, was recorded as a labourer.[60]

The first weeks in March saw a number of manoeuvres take place in advance of finally setting sail. These included unmooring and sailing short distances before stopping. On 2 March, when it appeared the ship was ready to sail, there was a spell of bad weather that prevented this. The captain's journal shows evidence that tensions rose in these final pre-sailing days, with some minor damage to bedclothes, squabbles between sailors and soldiers and the destruction of utensils. Finally, on 15 March, with the captain reporting that most of the convicts were sick; the *Chapman* departed Cork for New South Wales.[61]

2

Bloodshed in a Tropical Climate

The waters were unsettled in the days leading up to departure and this was not a naturally seafaring body of men. John Ennis crouched in a corner of the prison holding his stomach and groaning. The eighteen-year-old was now serving his sentence for the robbery on Bishop Street nine months earlier. As the *Chapman* manoeuvred out of the port, Ennis and his convict companions were overcome with a sickening anxiety about the ordeal that lay ahead. When the voyage got under way on 15 March, most of the convicts were sick. The bravado of the previous weeks anchored in Cove faded quickly as the claustrophobia of the timber prison walls swept across this cluster of men so odious in character that the law deemed that they were no longer fit to live in the country of their birth. Any man lucky enough to find himself on the outer deck was able to vomit over the side of the ship and into the waters below. For the convict remaining in the prison below he had no option but to tolerate the lingering stench of his own nauseous excretions and those of his cellmates.

Once at sea those parts of the *Chapman* visible from afar did not betray the fact that this was a floating prison. From the moment the last of the convicts were boarded in Cork those in control of the ship instigated their strict regime of only allowing the minimum number on deck for the shortest amount of time possible. On the prison deck of the ship were 200 men who had gradually experienced a reduction in their liberty and physical space during the previous months. This began with their detention in some police facility or other, having been apprehended for an offence for which they would be put on trial. Following that trial and conviction they were detained in a prison cell, not necessarily just in Kilmainham or Cork. Many shared cells before arriving on the *Chapman* and this very fact would later be put forward as a reason for distrusting the entire convict body on board. It is impossible to measure the range of emotions experienced by the men as they were placed on the ship in Cove during those final weeks before departure. A lot of them may not have even seen the sea, let alone been on board a ship that would carry them to an uncertain future. On the journey to that future, sons would be torn away from their parents, husbands from their wives, fathers from their children, men from their communities. A typically mild transgression resulted in an unprecedented sacrifice and there was a finality to this journey.

The industrial-scale transportation of convicts to New South Wales was all the more impressive due to the still unsophisticated nature of both the prison and shipping systems. The convicts lived and slept in an area of the ship formally designated as the prison. On most vessels this took up the entire space between decks, apart, possibly, for accommodation for certain officers or sailors. The prison was divided into spaces known as 'berths' and each one typically housed four convicts. Whenever possible, the convicts were allowed to air their bedding on deck every morning, where it was stored in netting in the event of sudden rainfall.[62] They were not to know that a combination of factors had already decreed that they would spend an unprecedented amount of the voyage in this tedious netherworld submerged beneath the surface of the ocean.

On the morning of the first full day at sea, Patrick Smith, one of the convicts, was removed from the prison and brought into the hospital. As he was ordered out to the adjoining sickbay the fifty-five-year-old Tyrone-born Smith had no idea why he was being singled out. His thoughts may have wandered back to 20 February the previous year when he appeared before Mr Justice Day at the City Commission in Dublin. After a detailed trial prosecuted using much forensic financial evidence, he was found guilty of feloniously uttering and selling a pack of cards, purporting to be a genuine pack, legally stamped, knowing them to be counterfeit. He was also convicted of possessing several other packs that he knew were forgeries. Smith's crime was non-violent but caused great offence among the upper echelons of Dublin society and their servants, many of whom were purchasers of the forged playing cards. Witnesses from the Excise Office and the Stamp Office testified to the specific nature of the forgeries. Smith was not without his supporters in court, with no fewer than four character witnesses. In sentencing the guilty man to seven years' transportation the judge declared this a 'monstrous, abominable and odious crime'. In fact, he regretted that this was not a crime that called for a capital sentence.

No longer in the comfort of his former home at 5 Molesworth Street in Dublin, Patrick Smith was marched into the sickbay. There he was allocated the position of doctor's mate for the duration of the voyage to New South Wales. When a convict was assigned such a responsibility he was given a degree of respite and at this early stage of the journey he could not possibly comprehend its value. Smith's new role allowed him to be on the deck at the same time as the sailors and gave him a unique insight into the running of the ship. More than this, it provided him with an escape, albeit limited, from the darkness and monotony of the prison below decks. Apart from his set duties as doctor's mate he could, of course, be called upon at any time to assist Surgeon Dewar. This brought a level of mental stimulation and access to fresh air that his cellmates could scarcely imagine after a few days below decks. Why was Patrick Smith chosen out of 200 convicted criminals as a suitable candidate for doctor's mate? At fifty-five he was somewhat older than the average available man. His crime was not one that caused physical harm to another individual. Crucially, in his previous life at the house on Molesworth Street, he was employed as a 'gentleman's servant'. His wife was also a servant. In Smith, Dewar and his fellow officers had identified a man who was trained to follow orders, carry out tasks and conditioned to make himself useful in the service of others. It was unlikely that he envisaged how useful he would need to be during the coming months.

While we are not informed of the layout and infrastructure of the hospital on the *Chapman*, we can use other convict transports from the immediate time period as a guide. The *Neptune* also sailed from England in 1817 and the hospital was equipped with a range of curiosities, some of which suggested a commitment to medical well-being and others that could be expected to be found anywhere on the vessel. These comprised of ten units each of duck frock, flannel trousers and waistcoats. In addition, there were twenty units each of pocket-handkerchiefs, night-caps and towels. There were thirty-four sheets and calico pillowcases. Pewter pans, urinals, spitting-pots, buckets, a bathing tub, a water purifier and an airing stove all combined to set the facility apart as a place of healing for the unwell and injured.[63] This distinguished it as a space for the treatment of the sick rather than just another place of detention in the floating prison.

The following day, 17 March, was a pivotal moment for the convicts when the ship's third mate, James Miles Baxter, was assigned to oversee the prison and its occupants. Among his duties was to ensure that both were clean. In her chapter comparing the fortunes of two so-called 'mutiny ships', the *Chapman* in 1817 and the *Tottenham* in 1818, Susan Ballyn questioned this decision, pointing out that it was a clear breach of the regulations under which the surgeon-superintendent was engaged. Dewar's role on the ship was a powerful one, extending to directing the captain to make an unscheduled stop on the journey to re-supply his medical equipment or attend to a sick convict. It was just a few days into the journey and some of this power was surrendered to Third Mate Baxter.[64] In the events that transpired during the subsequent months, no other figure loomed larger in the lives of the convicts than that of the notorious and hated Third Mate Baxter. From the beginning of the journey he did not hide his loathing for these men and gave them plenty of reason to reciprocate. Baxter was an experienced seafarer with a cruel streak and a booming voice, neither of which he was afraid to exercise. With the ship at sea and the officers and crew settling into their different roles, the following few days were quiet on board the *Chapman*.

The first alarm

On Saturday night, 22 March, and into the early hours of the following day the voyage experienced its first episode of disquiet. The sentinel at the fore hatchway raised an alarm to the effect that the convicts were picking the locks and attempting to make their way up on deck. In response, the soldiers and crew were immediately ordered to arm themselves in preparation for a defence of the ship. Captain Drake, Surgeon Dewar and Third Mate Baxter, made their way in the darkness down to the prison deck, where they found everything quiet. The soldiers and crew stood down from their armed posture, only to be recalled again at midnight when the alarm was sounded once more. Yet again there was no sign of anything untoward from the prison. Two crew members, Peter Cocker and Cornelius Crawley, were posted as sentinels to eavesdrop on the prisoners for the remainder of the night. Later they reported hearing whispers such as 'it's a bad job, we are found out' and 'the soldiers are not worth a damn'. They threatened to 'blow them all (the soldiers) to hell' if they had the chance. Others allegedly pointed out how there was plenty of time left.[65] Despite the fact that no convict was identified for wrongdoing in this incident, and, by extension, nobody was charged, the already suspicious captain and surgeon were rattled by a non-event. Whether it was the result of a nervous sentinel or some nefarious act from the prison, the seed of trepidation that was planted in the mind of Dewar by the commander of the *Atlas* in Cork many weeks earlier had now found its root.

The remainder of March was mostly uneventful. The convicts were mustered daily in different-sized groups on the outside deck. It was common for a man to find himself confined and handcuffed from 9 a.m. to 5.30 p.m. for insolence. As March turned into April and the journey continued deeper into the Atlantic, the weather improved considerably. The booming and unforgiving voice of Baxter was now an unrelenting presence across the ship and in the prison. Two hundred convicts had adjusted to life on the ocean and the effects on their bodies. On all nineteenth-century convict transports to Australia it was both customary and necessary to dock at a friendly port in order to re-supply the ship and possibly carry out any essential repairs. The *Chapman* was on a course to the Cape Verde island of Porto Praya and the port of St Jago. Although the Irish convicts would remain on the ship during this stopover, it nonetheless became a significant turning point towards the events that would unfold later in April. Men such as Ennis and Smith had never seen anything like this before.

Three nights in St Jago

On 4 April the ship anchored in Porto Praya and the soldiers and crew made their way into St Jago. The island was a Portuguese territory. The convicts remained on the ship but were mustered on the outdoor decks according to the wishes of the captain or third mate. As they stood or marched in the open air these petty criminals from the most impoverished districts of urban and rural Ireland were confronted by an awesome sight in the distance. The possibilities suggested by this stunning vista would remain unfulfilled. By coincidence, the exploratory vessel *Congo* also stopped at St Jago that same week. The commander, Captain Tuckey, later provided a detailed account of the setting encountered by his crew, and by extension, that of the *Chapman*. The town rested on a natural perpendicular platform with three rows of slum housing built with a combination of mud and stone. This layout was interspersed with bunches of date and palm trees.

As the sailors explored the town they too encountered a world that was sometimes as squalid as the one from which they emerged but one that was altogether more exotic than the dirge and industry of an English dockyard. Some of the houses were whitewashed and as a result stood out from the surrounding squalor. These structures were occupied in the main by senior military officers, who were entitled to take possession of any house they saw fit without having to recompense the existing residents. For this reason the locals kept their houses unattractive on purpose, so as to avoid their seizure for military use. A church, without a spire, blended into the urban landscape of St Jago, although it was probably more appropriate for occupation by cattle or lumber than as a place of worship.

As they gazed across the bay to the shoreline, the Irish convicts took turns marvelling at the structures that defended the bay at St Jago. There was nothing grandiose or remarkable about what they saw but it was exquisite. While they were accustomed to squalor in Ireland, this was squalor in a tropical climate, in an almost alien cultural setting. A fort-like structure housed sixteen old guns, which pointed out towards the sea and any unwanted visitors. They were mounted on a parapet wall that was almost in ruins. These defences were particularly weak, patrolled by a gang of unruly ruffian types who were apparently ill-prepared to do anything other than stand around in groups.

As they continued their adventure just beyond the perimeters of St Jago, the sailors found clusters of date trees and unstructured vegetation with no evidence of planned cultivation. There was a small cotton plantation and a number of wells which supplied water for the town and visiting ships. One onlooker noted that if the water was harnessed then it might bring much-needed industry to the island and make life more tolerable for the inhabitants of St Jago. He pointed out that it was unlikely that the Portuguese government would be capable of noticing such benefits. A deeper look at the island would show only coconut trees, sweet potatoes and cotton shrub in the best cultivated locations. Observers could see native women in states of near-nakedness but also considerable poverty. This was said to have dampened the spirits of eager male sailors from the *Congo* and *Chapman* during early April 1817. For the sailors and soldiers, but alas, not the convicts, they were tourists in what was for them a glorious and mysterious world.

There is some mystery about the specific activities of the crew and military guards of the *Chapman* during their three nights in St Jago. When the men left the ship, where record-keeping was a requirement, their activities were 'off-the-record'. Although just about two-and-a-half weeks into a four-month voyage, it is likely they sought whatever pleasures were offered in such a sparse and exotic environment. In an indication of a likely us-versus-them battle at sea, the soldiers and sailors from the ship engaged in a riot while on the island. In fact, most of the soldiers were 'in action' during the melee.[66]

Among the stock of supplies taken onboard by the *Chapman* before leaving the Cape Verde islands were livestock and fowl including cattle, sheep, goats, pigs, turkeys and hens. They also took on board fruit and water. Visiting sailors typically wanted to purchase some of the many green monkeys they had been offered but this was forbidden by their captain.[67] One purchase that became an issue some days later was the supply of St Jago beef that would serve the needs of those on board for the remaining months, but it is not clear if this was 'on the hoof' or processed. The *Chapman* weighed anchor and departed St Jago for a non-stop journey to New South Wales on 7 April. Porto Praya, with its rich landscape and intriguing possibilities, faded into the background, only to be replaced by a sense of gloom, tension and inevitable tragedy.

The Porto Praya beef and other tensions at sea
When the *Chapman* sailed away from Porto Praya neither the crew nor the passengers would see land again until late July. The break in the normal routine upset the stability that marked the voyage thus far. The convicts and the sailors became somewhat more emboldened. Relationships had now been formed and suspicions began to develop on all sides. Soon after the journey resumed, Baxter visited Dewar in his quarters. The third mate was somewhat incensed because convicts were refusing to carry out one of their key assigned duties, which was to dry holystone the deck. This was a cleaning process using a block of sandstone to sand the deck of a ship. Ultimate responsibility for ordering these cleaning routines rested with the surgeon but on the *Chapman* it was Baxter who was designated to ensure it was carried out. Dewar went to the convicts and was convinced by their (unstated) grievances to the point that he complied with their wishes.

The officers noticed that almost immediately after this part of the voyage began, the convicts became more insolent and disorderly. When they were in the prison the men were chained in irons and these shackles were a permanent feature of life at sea. They were a control mechanism designed to slow down the progress of the already locked-down body of men. It was at this time that the crew alleged that the rivets holding the irons in place were tampered with, broken or were deficient. Several convicts later admitted that these observations were correct but claimed that the restraints were merely loosened to allow them to dress and wash with greater ease. After all, the convicts lived out almost every aspect of their journey within the confines of the prison. They ate, cleaned and slept in this crowded and unsanitary place. The least they felt they needed was the ability to manoeuvre their limbs. While this was accepted as reasonable *after* the voyage, in the midst of the isolation and vulnerability of the sea it served to heighten tensions among an increasingly suspicious crew.

Surgeon Dewar claimed he visited the hospital every morning after breakfast and usually one or two more times throughout the day. He would later be heard to boast that he was one of the best friends the convicts had on the ship, someone who was kind, available to provide medical attention at all hours, a man who listened to grievances and provided swift redress. If this was correct then his brand of military medicine would have been almost unique during that era. Almost 140 years later he unfathomably remained somewhat of a legend in the Australian press, where he was described as 'a lazy, elderly naval surgeon'.[68] He also declared that the convicts were well treated up to this point of the journey. They were satisfied with their rations, felt safe and were unthreatened by any individual. This is not supported by the prevailing feelings of all on board towards the foreboding figure of the menacing Third Mate Baxter, perhaps the only officer who struck genuine fear into the convicts. As the tensions continued to rise in the days after leaving St Jago, so too did the wrath of the most terrifying gaoler on the ship.

The friction continued to grow during the following days. On the afternoon of 12 April, convict John Jackson came to Surgeon Dewar in the sickbay. Jackson was a twenty-two-year-old Limerick native. In August of the previous year he was convicted of stealing a writing desk and £300 in Bank of Ireland tokens from Lieutenant Colonel McManus of the Antrim Regiment of Militias, and £700 from Alexander O'Hara, Acting Paymaster of the same unit.[69] Such a crime should almost certainly have warranted execution yet eight months later Jackson found himself on the *Chapman* in front of the surgeon as convict representative on all matters related to food quality and rations. He was instructed to inform the doctor that the convicts would not be accepting fresh beef the following day. The reasons were not recorded. Dewar replied that fresh beef would indeed be served. The men argued the issue for a short time but the surgeon's word was final on such affairs and Jackson departed the sickbay to relate the unhappy news. The following morning one of the convicts' cooks sent a message announcing that they would reject the fresh beef. Still Dewar persisted and the meat was served. To add to Dewar's problems, the sailors also refused to eat what was noted in official logs as the 'Porto Praya beef'. The surgeon and officer of the guard deemed it good and wholesome. The sailors found common ground with the prisoners and both had lost this minor skirmish with the officers. Was it possible that the rejection of the Porto Praya beef by the sailors and the prisoners, two groups prohibited from communicating with each other, was purely coincidental, or could this have been a coordinated effort?

Nelson and Crawley

At around seven o'clock on the evening of 12 April, William Nelson, one of the sailors, was found lurking in the main hatchway near the prison by a sentinel on duty. Nelson was not supposed to be in that location at that time and because of this he fled in a hurry after being confronted by the man who was on duty. The crew and guard were all put on armed alert because the soldier, not being familiar with Nelson, believed that one of the convicts had escaped. Cornelius Crawley, another sailor, told Captain Drake that one man exited the prison through the chain-scuttle while others were already running up the ships' rigging. Surgeon Dewar, who was in the cuddy with the officer of the guard and the captain's brother, John Drake, emerged on deck, where he was confronted by an incident that had escalated into a chaotic state of noise and confusion. Soldiers with lanterns searched the ship from top to bottom. Third Mate Baxter stalked the decks barking orders at his frightened subordinates. Musket shots were fired into the rigging. Before long the true identity of the figure in the hatchway was discovered and calm was restored.

In the immediate aftermath of the tussle a new target for suspicion emerged and this time it was not any of the convicts. The sailors Nelson and Crawley were accused by some of their fellow crew members of being too cosy with the prisoners. When questioned about his presence in the hatchway near the prison, Nelson replied that he was fetching water. His interrogators rejected this claim on the basis that there were several other locations across the ship from which he could get water, rather than this one from which he was expressly forbidden to enter. One of the problems with Nelson being in this hatchway was that it allowed easy communication into the prison. As a result of what the captain believed was a lame explanation, coupled with the suspicions of their colleagues, both Nelson and Crawley were placed in irons for the night.

The following morning, Nelson was brought before his accusers on the outer deck, where a charge was read against him. Neither the specific punishment not the wording of the charge are recorded; however, the general thrust of the accusation focussed on the extent of his communication with the convicts. Both he and Crawley readily acknowledged that they were well-disposed towards the convicts. Nelson was seen as the greater menace because of a previous incident in which one of the convicts, Francis Murphy, allegedly tried to obtain his keys with a view to ultimately accessing the gun room. In August 1816 at the Louth Assizes, Murphy was convicted of stealing four banknotes and sentenced to seven years' transportation.[70] There was no evidence that Nelson ever reported Murphy's surreptitious behaviour to the officers of the ship.

On top of this was an allegation that Nelson was aware of a convict plot to take the ship. It was alleged that he had heard Crawley discussing this more than once and that he also witnessed convicts swearing each other in to the conspiracy. It later emerged that Nelson had actually informed Captain Drake of this at the time. It was suspected that Nelson and Crawley were in regular contact with two convicts, Collins and Jackson, and discussed this plot. Twenty-year-old Francis Murphy was said to have sworn Crawley into the conspiracy. His task would be to open the prison doors while the officers were at dinner. Crawley denied all of this while Jackson claimed it was true. Another sailor named White was also identified as being too close to the convicts. At this point the only one physically punished was Nelson who, along with Crawley and White, was placed in irons.

The exact nature of what was happening during these particular days was widely disputed by all concerned for years after the voyage ended. What is patently obvious is that there was a conspiracy to disrupt the voyage. The exact nature of the conspiracy is not as clear-cut. Was it being formed among the convicts, or the sailors, or both? Was it idle talk and swagger that probably happened on every convict voyage with no proper intention of executing any plan? Or was there a much more low-key and hitherto unseen force at work, one that was ready to show its hand?

The alleged conspiracy

By 16 April, the convict William Leo found himself confined to the orlop (lowest) deck for suspicious and insolent conduct. He joined Michael Savage, John Jackson and Edward Donoughoe, who were already detained on similar charges. While in custody, Donoghue was alleged to have said 'I'll fight till I die'. This was later seen as contributing to the overall deteriorating atmosphere on board. Why such a statement from a poorly educated petty criminal who spent most of the past month in a lower-deck prison dungeon would have seemed so threatening is unclear.

The voyage that same day was marred by heavy rain, meaning that no convict could go out on deck until at least mid-afternoon. These days were always the most dismal in the prison. The knowledge that the usual routine of liberating small groups of men in turn was at a standstill added to the misery and tedium because it meant that nothing would change all day. Nobody would leave and, therefore, nobody would return with stories of what might have happened on the outermost deck. Apprehension rose to such a level that Captain Drake ordered that a chain cable be placed across the main hatchway to further secure the prison.

Between two and three o'clock that same afternoon the convicts were mustered on deck as a security measure. The crew and guard were all armed and in a state of readiness for some unforeseen hostile action. A total of eighty-three sets of irons were found to be defective and this did nothing to quell the sense of threat now felt by the officers. It was during this exercise that one of the key players in the story of the voyage made his move. The convict Michael Collins whispered to Third Mate Baxter that a general conspiracy was now active among his fellow prisoners. Twenty-six-year-old Collins was a native of Bantry in County Cork. In 1815 or 1816 he was convicted of the theft of a pack containing soft goods worth more than £27 from a pedlar named Mathew Sullivan.[71] This was another of those offences where the guilty man was lucky to escape with his life. Collins was sent back down to the prison without incident while Baxter reported the claim to the captain and other senior officers.

Dewar believed that the information was fully in keeping with everything he and his colleagues had experienced of late. Between untrustworthy sailors and insolent convicts with their broken irons a picture was forming. The time had come to place the vessel in a state of readiness. Such was the extent of the alarm caused by this specific intelligence, Drake decided to pass the chain cable over the fore and after hatchways and to bring the arms-chest and all other weapons up onto the poop deck. With soldiers and crew seemingly prepared for battle it was decided to allow sixty prisoners – twelve per hour – up on deck during the remaining daylight hours. When darkness came, the night watch was put in place and on 16 April the *Chapman* enjoyed her last peaceful night at sea.

The alleged mutiny of the *Chapman* was scheduled to take place on the second day after departing the island of St Jago following a routine stopover. Michael Collins claimed that one of the convicts, Francis Murphy, approached him with news of the plot. Under this carefully orchestrated coup, every convict was required to take an oath to the plot. Murphy allegedly ordered:

> Collins, come out here and be sworn, as I am myself, to be staunch and loyal, not to deceive each other; for it's our determination to take the ship and put every soul to death; the time fixed for the attempt is twelve o'clock on Sunday night, and Hugh Maloy is to be the password. The First Mate's life is to be spared until we get in sight of land, when he is to be killed.

'I would sooner be shot,' responded Collins. Another alleged conspirator, Peter Allen, intervened and asked Murphy why he did not 'split me [Collins] open with a knife'. Collins relented and took the oath. All of those who took the oath swore to be loyal and not to deceive each other, as it was the convicts' intention to take the ship and murder the crew and guard and everyone on board, except the chief mate.

The ringleaders, according to Collins, even went so far as to plan a new crew from within their own ranks. One of the convicts, named Flynn, was to be the captain's brother and 'sailing captain'.[72] John Morrison would be the captain, Murphy the doctor, McLean the officer of the guard and Peter Allen the first mate. It was planned that all of these, presumably eminently unqualified, new officers would wear the uniforms of their predecessors. Under the plan the new team of prisoner-officers intended to keep 100 convicts in irons on the outer decks during the day or in the prison at night in the event that the ship was sighted or boarded by any other vessel at sea. This was quite possible because the convict ship the *Pilot* left Cove around the same time as the *Chapman*. They would even have new ship's books containing the names of the hundred men in irons, along with those of the new officers.

The taking of an oath was a key part of the mutiny strategy. Bearing in mind that the overwhelming majority of the convicts were likely Roman

Catholic and Irish, they had an almost iron-clad relationship to their faith. An oath was seen as a security mechanism to lock down the participation of any man involved in the plot. Collins reported that all the captains of the messes in the prison took the oath. In fact, he and three others, Murphy, Morrison and Allen, were designated to oblige the taking of the oath. No convict refused, for the consequences of this would be stark. Any uncooperative prisoner would be smothered with blankets, quartered, and removed from the ship in pieces through the port holes.

Collins confirmed the officers' suspicions about the behaviour of some of the sailors. He revealed that Nelson and Crawley had already provided two bars of iron, two knives, a hammer and long nails to the prisoners. Convicts Murphy, Allen and McLean were designated to receive these items at the prison door of the main hatchway. This equipment was to be added to lengths of wood to be found inside the prison and fashioned into spears and other sharp weapons. The first victims of these weapons were already identified, according to the Collins version of the plot. Third Mate Baxter would be murdered for being too severe. Fourth Mate Campion would be killed for not giving water to the prisoners when they needed it. The carpenter's mate was in the crosshairs of the prisoners for refusing to provide nails.

A detailed plan was devised and the ringleaders created the password 'Hugh Maloy' as an extra layer of security for themselves. A group of convicts would force open the fore scuttle to attract the attention of everyone on deck. Once this was achieved the main body of men would rush the scene and make their way to the guard room, where they would seize any available firearms. From there they would go to the powder room, which they would set on fire if they could not make their way back to the deck. They concluded it would be better to be blown up rather than shot by the guards. Thursday 17 April was the day selected for the mutiny according to Collins, because the ship was at the point of shortest passage to America. How he believed the convicts knew this information is not clear.

Somehow the plan was rescheduled to the following day when a group of men, apparently selected by the convicts themselves, were allowed up on deck to wash. The stoutest men from within the prison were selected, along with three cooks and four swabbers. Altogether twenty-four men were to keep watch while on deck and as soon as the officers retired for dinner they were to disable the sentinels, take possession of the quarter deck and commence the attack as outlined. As a reward for their endeavours the mutineers planned a feast for the entire convict population of the *Chapman* the following day. A dinner consisting of roast turkey, pigs and geese, with a glass of brandy after the goose, followed by Port and Madeira wine, would mark the beginning of a new and unplanned chapter of the voyage.

The final day of peace

The first muster of the convicts on Thursday, 17 April took place in the morning. All of the men were brought up on deck, where their irons were inspected. Many of the fixtures were again discovered to be broken or deficient. A sense of foreboding now consumed the crew at every level. Captain Drake was drinking heavily most evenings and nights while Surgeon Dewar had palmed off most of his non-medical duties to the hated Third Mate Baxter, who welcomed any extra power. Even worse was the level of distrust that was developing between these officers and the ordinary sailors that comprised the lost ranks of the crew. As soon as the first muster was concluded, Michael Collins was brought before the officers of the ship to give a full account of his conspiracy theory. The reaction was swift. The first mate left the meeting before Collins finished speaking to begin circulating word among the entire crew, as well as to adopt other defensive measures. After telling his story, the twenty-six-year-old Bandon native was hailed by the officers as the 'preserver of the ship' and immediately taken into protective custody.

Surgeon Dewar's first instinct took him back to the sickbay, where two prisoners happened to be isolated for medical reasons. He forcefully interrogated the men in an attempt to corroborate the details presented by Collins but they denied any knowledge of the alleged mutiny plot. Meanwhile the other officers imposed the usual fortification procedures, which included a chain passed through and interlinked with the existing chain cable over the different hatchways. Arms and ammunition were also put at the ready. Whether Collins divulged this story because it was true or because he wanted to curry favour, by convincing the officers of the existence of a plot he transformed a highly unstable and dangerous atmosphere into a potentially lethal crisis.

A second muster was called at four o'clock in the afternoon and the sound of drum beats called the crew and soldiers to arms. Drake and Dewar claimed that an even greater number of irons were broken or tampered with since the morning muster. Five or six of the convicts received corporal punishment due to the state of their irons. The still-imprisoned sailor, Crawley, received thirty-six lashes for suspicious behaviour while the twenty-five-year-old convict James Fox escaped punishment because he surrendered a file that was known to be somewhere in the prison. As the well-practised routine ended and all personnel, criminal or otherwise, returned to their stations or quarters, this was the final muster involving all of the prisoners that departed from Cork over a month earlier. The fuse was ready. All that remained was to wait for the spark.

'Fire away boys, kill all the bloody bastards!'

As the *Chapman* sailed into another night all was quiet in the prison. Most of those in the prison were in bed. According to one of the convicts, Terence Kiernan, a few were in the roundhouse (he presumably meant a separate confinement facility on board the ship). The prisoners were quiet and anxious to get to bed. There was nothing to suggest that this thirty-fourth night on the Atlantic Ocean would be any different from all that went before. At eight o'clock in the evening, Captain Drake was walking on the quarter deck. A later published account claimed that he was drunk in his cabin when tensions fully escalated on the ship.[73] Surgeon Dewar was sitting in the cuddy with Lieutenant Busteed and John Drake, the captain's brother. Thomas Turner, one of the soldiers, later recounted how he was on duty between six and eight o'clock that evening. His instructions were no different from any other night; he was free to fire his weapon if the convicts attempted to break out. At one point he heard noises from below and called down 'to know what was the matter, but received no answer'.[74] The ship's cook, James Wells, was standing on the grate of the starboard forescuttle when he claimed he felt it lifting under him. An alarm was sounded across the ship to the effect that the convicts were attempting to break free from the prison. The escalation was swift and violent. The fuse was lit.

Captain Drake made his way to the scene but found all was quiet. He claimed that moments later, while standing by the starboard gangway near the main hatchway, he heard the rushing of feet inside the prison. Terence Kiernan was in his bed, which was located towards the front of the ship, in the prison. He made no mention of anyone inside the prison attempting to force open a grate. He could hear Third Mate Baxter at the forescuttle roaring into the prison before ramming his cutlass (a type of short sword used by sailors) into the opening. He later swore that at this moment there was a huge rush of convicts away from this part of the prison towards the back and out of harm's way. At that moment the first shooting commenced. Kiernan claimed all but one of the convicts were still wearing their leg irons.

Dewar, Busteed and Drake emerged out on deck at the sound of gunfire. The ship descended into a floating quagmire of fear and confusion. The surgeon had a difficult time ascertaining exactly what was happening. Some sailors told him that the prisoners were forcing the scuttles and coming forward and others claimed that they had escaped the prison through the hospital door and were already on the attack. Dewar later concluded that the initial chaos was caused by the belief that the treacherous nature of the now-detained sailors Crawley and Nelson could have spread to others in the crew. The suspicion that was once held only towards the convicts now included most of the sailors and soldiers and proved incendiary at this moment.

Sailors and soldiers rushed around the decks in all states of undress, for many had been in their sleeping quarters. Muskets were brought out of their secure storage rooms and loaded. Terror and confusion reigned above and below deck. In the prison the only available light was provided through the scuttle and the hatchways. Kiernan saw Baxter appear at the after hatchway, where he fired several musket shots into the prison. The reviled third mate ordered his soldiers to continue loading their weapons. Kiernan shielded himself using the timbers of his bed. 'Fire away boys,' roared Baxter, 'kill all the bloody bastards!' He later swore that he implored upon the mutineers to surrender, but they refused.[75] Kiernan estimated the firing went on for the next hour-and-a-half. He described how the prisoners began crying for mercy from the fourth or fifth shot onwards but their attackers showed no restraint. Patrick Smith, the surgeon's mate and one of the convicts, was in the sickbay when the shooting began. He later testified that the prison had been perfectly quiet during the time immediately before the shooting began. As it progressed, the musket shots appeared to come from different directions. Convicts were wounded from the beginning, including the man next to Kiernan. The prison lapsed into a state of disorientation.

As the shooting continued, Baxter directed musket fire in the direction of any cries for mercy. He allegedly told his soldiers that these were not cries for mercy but declarations to give no quarters to the attackers. The convicts, in return, should be given no quarters. After a ten-minute ceasefire the shooting restarted and Baxter appeared at the after hatchway. Roaring into the prison he vowed he would 'kill every bloody bugger', before firing at least two shots. He warned the convicts that he knew every inch of the prison, that essentially, they had nowhere to hide. The fear was intense and fevered. The moaning of wounded and dying convicts was all that could be heard in those rare moments when the gunfire stopped. The only ship's officer to be seen or heard from within the prison was Baxter. When the attack ceased, the prisoners could hear Surgeon Dewar overhead. Kiernan did not know any of the soldiers by name and found it difficult to identify their faces in the darkness and pandemonium.

Most accounts of the parallel events above the prison agree that the attack was disordered and shambolic. Drake, Dewar and Busteed continued in their attempts to ascertain the status of the prisoners and the threat to the ship. As they realised that the convicts were indeed safely incarcerated in the prison they attempted to bring a halt to the firing, but to no avail. According to Dewar, the soldiers and sailors were so animated and agitated by the situation that they could not be reasoned with or restrained. Surgeon's Mate Patrick Smith confirmed he heard Drake attempting to stop the shooting. The soldier Thomas Turner later confirmed that nobody on deck was aware at that point whether the ship was under the control of the crew or the convicts. At that moment it became clear that Captain John Drake was not in control of the *Chapman*.

The seven-to-ten-minute respite unexpectedly took place because one of the sailors was accidentally shot dead in the crossfire. He may well have been the first person to die on the voyage. The next phase of shooting lasted for between ten and fifteen minutes. Most accounts agree that at this point the convicts were asked for, or offered, quarters, and submitted accordingly. Once they kneeled around the hatchway and prayed for their lives the firing stopped. Two of the most detailed convict explanations agree, however, that the cries for mercy began from after the fourth or fifth shot but were ignored by a bloodthirsty Third Mate Baxter. There is every possibility that in the midst of the firing and shouting that was overwhelming the ship during those moments, it may not have been possible for Baxter and his soldiers to hear the early pleas for mercy.

★

As the *Chapman* sailed quietly through dark waters parallel to the coast of West Africa, nobody came to attend to the dead or wounded that night. After the shooting ended and the mass adrenalin rush of the previous hour slowed down to a normal pace, the horror continued in the prison. In almost total darkness the unharmed convicts could scarcely figure out how many among their own number were wounded or killed. The groans of anguish and suffering were heard all through the long night as dead and maimed petty criminals lay helpless and unattended among their terrified cell-mates. Even among the very worst of them, none had ever experienced anything like the nightmar-ish vision of hell that pervaded their prison that night. They were only distracted from the stench of urine, excrement and blood by their own painful whimpering. Though they controlled the soldiers and the fire-arms, Captain Drake and Surgeon Dewar took the cowardly decision not to come to the aid of the fallen convicts during the night. This was a misjudgement. Even though the terms of their employment required them to enter the prison at any time of the day or night when medical attention was needed, they remained above decks, fearful of a reprisal from the convicts. Dewar was later heard to say that it was not deemed safe to open the prison that night, and 'if I myself had been willing to make the risk, I could have found no one hardy enough to have accompanied or assist me'.[76] In fact, the sole assurance the convicts received during that night came from the sentries guarding them from the outside. They would shoot any man that gave further trouble. As sailors cowered in their stations around the ship and armed soldiers patrolled the decks, the mournful sounds continued from the prison, where the living prayed for a respite from the horror that could only be provided by the coming of daylight.

3

Escalation

Although the day was fine and bright, the light did not flood into the prison the next morning. In fact, the prison was never fully bathed in any kind of light. Some fragments of the day were always evident through the timbers or different scuttle-holes but depending on their location most prisoners only knew the darkness, whatever the hour. In fact, the steadiest form of lighting was provided by candles, but even this was limited. At daybreak on 18 April those tiny fissures between the timbers illuminated only the blood of fallen convicts. The cries of the wounded had died down by morning to be replaced by the low and unrelenting hum of groaning and pain. Those who were physically untouched by the gunfire of the night persevered by maintaining a terrified silence. As morning broke, the voice of Third Mate James Baxter could once again be heard thundering on the external perimeters of the prison and many of the men were so disoriented that they were unsure of his exact location. He seemed to be everywhere.

Sometime after dawn a soldier knocked at the prison door with a message. The prisoners were ordered to send up any contraband material that might serve as a weapon. If the suspicious objects were not produced immediately the messenger promised that the shooting would recommence and not finish until every man in the prison was dead. At this point, none of the officers, soldiers or sailors had yet entered the prison since the men were locked in and fired upon during the night.

The prisoners begged for some time in order to search their quarters and find any offending items. This was granted and some minutes later a small number of files and saws were produced to the soldiers. The officers discovered that the stockpile of weapons produced was so tiny that even in the hands of the convicts it posed no threat to the ship, although some soldiers claimed to have seen files and irons thrown from the prison scuttles and into the sea during this search process. In any event, with the authorities satisfied that the convicts were disarmed they decided that the time had come to enter the prison.

The prison becomes a mortuary

As they prepared to descend the hatchway into the prison, Captain Drake and Surgeon Dewar were themselves very much at the mercy of Baxter. The volatile third mate appeared to relish his starring role managing the aftermath of the crisis and snarled orders at sailors and soldiers alike, although he did not have authority over the latter. Drake was genuinely concerned at Baxter's behaviour during this period because his incendiary language and tone seemed to be having the effect of creating some form of uprising among the crew and guards. Twice he was ordered out of the hatchway by Drake and in the turmoil of the moment he refused both times. Once more the captain felt that control of the *Chapman* was slipping beyond his grip and James Miles Baxter was to blame.

Eventually, Drake and Dewar, accompanied by Baxter and a number of soldiers and sailors, entered the prison to survey the outcome of the musket fire of the previous night. What they found was a massacre. Thirty-five-year-old George Stephenson was on this voyage because he was convicted of stealing money in his native Belfast. Now he lay dead on the floor of the ship, a victim of indiscriminate gunfire at the hands of Baxter or one of the soldiers. Loughlin McCleare was thirty and also from Belfast. Convicted of robbery, he too would not see New South Wales. The third fatality was twenty-eight-year-old house robber Daniel McCormick, from Sligo. Did these men suffer through the night before succumbing to their death, or were they killed instantly? These facts are not known. What is clear is that theirs was not the only suffering endured because of the shooting.

As the visitors made their way deeper into the prison the full extent of the disaster became apparent. 'Why, damned my soul,' declared Baxter, puffing up his chest, 'there is but very few of them killed.' The convicts cowered in their messes, some in fear and others showing expressions of defiance. Twenty-two men were wounded and lay in various states of pain around the floors. A few were in a serious condition and they too would not reach New South Wales. Neither Baxter nor Dewar were in a sympathetic mood as they surveyed the grisly sight of blood and tissue scattered across the prison. Baxter ordered that the dead be carried up by men from their own mess. Some of the sailors went to the aid of a wounded prisoner and Dewar, pointing his finger towards a corner, growled at them to 'throw him there'.

Terence Kiernan was one of the many uninjured convicts looking on as Drake, Dewar and Baxter prowled the prison deck, emboldened only by the protection of soldiers and sailors armed with guns and cutlasses. Kiernan was not sure that Baxter even needed such protection, given that he possessed such a ferocious character and menacing demeanour. Once they investigated the state of disarray among the convicts the three senior officers huddled together as they plotted the next steps. Even in whispers, Baxter's voice was heard above the others and his hand gestures would lead an outsider to believe that he was the one in command of the ship at that moment and not Captain Drake. When the discussion broke up the officers had formulated a strategy. Baxter delivered his orders to the soldiers and sailors. A new and even more horrific phase of life on board the *Chapman* had been plotted. Retribution was at hand.

Punishing the 'conspirators'

Five men were initially identified to face the wrath of all the ranks of the ship from top to bottom, by now baying for convict blood. Their designation as the ringleaders or the conspirators was the result of the interchange between Drake, Dewar and Baxter. The third mate and his crew were firmly in charge of the punishments to come. James Burns was a nineteen-year-old carpentry apprentice and pig-stealer from Wexford. Secondly came James Murray, a thirty-eight-year-old fraudster from Longford. In August 1816, twenty-year-old butcher Francis Murphy was convicted of stealing four banknotes at Ardee, County Louth.[77] Now, six months later, he joined others awaiting his fate on the outer deck of the *Chapman*. The next convict selected for punishment was William Leo, already firmly in the crosshairs of the officers and crew. Finally, twenty-year-old William Connor from Dublin, convicted of stealing nine small towels from Eleanor Cavanagh the previous July, was also led to a potentially deadly fate.[78]

Ironically, all accounts of these moments agree that it was the crew and soldiers of the ship, rather than the prisoners, who were in a mutinous state. The five prisoners were hauled up on deck, where the sailors and soldiers had appointed themselves judge and jury. They collectively agreed that the men should immediately be shot. Such was the heightened state of tension on the ship and loss of control by the captain, that the crew and soldiers were ready to begin executing prisoners for what was a false alarm the previous night. If they had their way, Burns, Murray, Murphy, Leo and Connor would only be the beginning. The most chilling proposition came from one quarter and suggested that one prisoner from each of the seventeen messes should be taken up and shot, as an example. This was not accepted.

Two or three of the men were placed on their knees in preparation for their final moments. Hoods were placed over their heads. The officers looked on in horror at what they later claimed was a punishment that did not fit the crime. A lengthy stand-off began where Drake and Dewar worked to change the minds of the sailors and soldiers. Eventually the senior men prevailed but only after promising to severely punish the men on the deck. According to the officer of the guard, 'the men were punished to quiet the minds of the soldiers and sailors, or otherwise they would have taken the lives of the prisoners, they were so inflamed.' He did not believe Surgeon Dewar would have sanctioned the corporal punishments otherwise.[79] As part of this dubious agreement it was decided that punishing the original five 'ringleaders' would not be sufficient.

They were joined by six other convicts hauled up from the prison. The floggings were carried out one prisoner at a time in a gruesome spectacle played out at sea. Barnard Kelly was given thirty-six lashes on the back. William Grady received twenty-six, William Connor twenty-four, William Leo thirty-six, Thomas Magiff thirty, John Doyal [*sic*] eight,

Francis Murphy seventeen, John Flood twenty-four, Edward Donoghoe thirty, Michael Savage thirty-six, and the sailor, William Nelson, twenty-four. James Burns, one of the five originally brought up for execution, was given thirty-six lashes. While he was being punished by the boatswain, Third Mate Baxter became impatient, took off his shirt, grabbed the flogging device and administered the final thirty lashes himself. He claimed that his subordinate was neither quick nor forceful enough with the punishment. Although he was almost faint from his punishment, Burns was taken down and handcuffed by Surgeon Dewar. Despite being almost crippled from the ordeal, the handcuffs remained in place until the following morning.

Investigators later decided that the manner in which the officers succumbed to the will of the crew and soldiers in this incident changed the fate of the prisoners for the remainder of the voyage to New South Wales. The brutality of the floggings was tolerated because the crew and guard believed that they were administering a punishment that should have been capital rather than corporal; in other words, the flogged prisoners were getting off lightly and enduring much less than they deserved. Much to the detriment of the prisoners, all personnel on the ship from that moment 'continued to make them the subjects of miserable distress, coercion and cruel treatment'.[80] The corporal punishments were concluded by the end of that morning but the full horror of that day had not yet been realised.

The grim task of attending to the dead was yet to be undertaken. Three convicts and a sailor lost their lives in the gunfire of the previous night but that horror was temporarily replaced by the panic and screams of flogged prisoners throughout the following sunny morning. In the afternoon the bodies of the convicts George Stephenson, Daniel McCormick and Lauchlan McLean, as well as that of the sailor John Murray, were all committed to the sea. In keeping with maritime practice of the time, their remains would not continue the voyage to Sydney. The casting of a corpse into the deep ocean was not borne out of tradition as much as it was of necessity. If a body was kept on the ship beyond a period of a few hours it posed a real danger to the health of all on board due to a combination of the lack of appropriate storage conditions and the hot climate.[81] As it was, all of the prisoners on the *Chapman* had already spent a night in a poorly ventilated timber dungeon with three corpses. Nautical super-stition also dictated that keeping a corpse on a ship would attract bad weather or slow down the voyage. If this arose then the body should be cast overboard immediately. During the nineteenth-century in the British Navy it was typical to sew the deceased person into their ham-mock before releasing their body to the depths, and it can be assumed that similar processes were used on this occasion.[82]

Once the burials were dealt with it was necessary to tend to the injured convicts in the prison. The twenty-two men had their wounds treated and dressed. The final step toward eliminating the visible manifestations of the slaughter was to clean the prison deck. After this was concluded the facility was sprinkled with vinegar, the favoured disinfectant under such circumstances.

The persecution of a 'perjured rascal'

One of the original five convicts brought up from the prison for corpo-ral punishment was already someone who roused contempt among the crew at all ranks. After being hauled into the sunlight by Baxter's men, William Leo was told by Dr Dewar that he was one of the ringleaders; a damned rascal. Although he had already spent time as a prisoner on the poop deck, Leo had not yet been charged with an offence on the voyage and, therefore, had never experienced corporal punishment. The surgeon took the thirty-seven-year-old aside and asked if he would confess to the existence of a plot to take the ship and the lives of the crew. Dewar made it clear that if he confessed, his life would be spared. If he refused to confess, he would be shot. With his shirt over his head to cover his face, Leo was placed on his hands and knees. 'I said it is of no use to deny it. If I swear it to you will you not believe me? You called me a perjured rascal and I'll die innocent.'[83]

'He is a hardened wretch,' declared the surgeon grimly. 'He will not tell of the rest. Take him up and give him a damned good flogging.' William Leo was given thirty-six lashes and once more the impatient Third Mate Baxter intervened with the boatswain to administer the punishment himself.

Although Drake and Dewar later claimed that the crew was responsible for leading the charge of punishments against the convicts that morning, it still fell to the surgeon and third mate to give the orders. Dewar had no problem indulging the worst extremes of the bloodlust of his sailors and soldiers, and it fell to William Leo to absorb those excesses. Once the flogging was concluded the surgeon ordered that a pickle known as brine be rubbed across his back, lavishly applied to the wounds. If the purpose of this was to cause excruciating pain to the victim, it succeeded. The prisoner, already smarting from a degree of pain he had not previously experienced, screamed in agony. But the sailors were not finished.

Dewar brazenly claimed later that he did not witness what happened next because he was busy overseeing the punishment of other convicts. Leo's tormentors tied a large rope around his torso and cast him over the side of the ship. As he was hanging above the water they pricked him with bayonets. He later claimed that he heard the sergeant of the guard say that this was 'a bad use of a person' who had already been punished and he ordered them to desist. As William Leo hung by a rope over the side of a ship crossing faraway seas it is unlikely that his mind went back to that night in Belvedere Place in Dublin the previous June. When he stole the horse brasses and harnesses of Mrs Blennerhasset, he could not have foreseen his present predicament.

The *Chapman* continued to sail with William Leo hanging over the side. With the sailors and soldiers jeering from above, he was dropped in and out of the water ten or eleven times. As the seawater mixed with the brine against his wounds the Galway-born criminal drifted in and out of consciousness, almost unaware of his own fear of drowning. His awareness of time also drifted away. It seemed to go on forever but in reality his ordeal probably lasted a few minutes. All the time, he remained handcuffed.

Leo was withdrawn from the water and returned to the safety of the ship. He was transferred to the orlop deck, where he remained until seven or eight o'clock the next morning. Under the supervision of Dr Dewar, he was taken back up on deck for another round of interrogation. Had he anything further to say about the prisoners and a possible plot that might save his life? 'I know nothing about it,' he protested. The captain rewarded this answer with two strong blows to the jaw.

'You hardened villain,' roared Drake. 'You must have been sworn below amongst the rest or else you would tell me.' Leo was once again in fear for his life but for now he was detained yet again on the poop deck along with three other prisoners. The men were placed in double irons with a chain running through the loops for additional security. 'There you will remain, rain, cold or snow, until you arrive at New South Wales,' threatened Drake. 'For I would as soon have your names as yourselves alive.'

During his remaining time imprisoned on the poop deck, Leo was flogged on two or three further occasions. During one of those events, by his own admission, he could take no more of the cat-o'-nine-tails and decided to confess that he was indeed aware of a plot to take the ship. He was removed to the cuddy and brought before Surgeon Dewar, who directed that he should suffer no further punishment. Dewar asked Leo which convict was to be appointed captain following the supposed mutiny on the *Chapman* but he did not know. William Leo had been brutally broken by his jailors and decided to answer 'yes' to all of Dewar's subsequent questions. 'Was Morrison not supposed to be captain?' 'Yes Sir.' 'Was Murphy not supposed to be the doctor?' 'Yes Sir.' Dewar took copious notes as Leo finally provided some answers, but later claimed that these were merely lies designed to avoid further punishment. With his interrogation completed the prisoner was returned to the poop deck where he expected, but did not receive, another flogging. This part of his ordeal was now over.

Getting the story straight

Burying the dead. Tending to the wounded. Cleaning out the prison. There was much to be done in the aftermath of the night of 17 April. Parallel to all of this and behind closed doors on those parts of the *Chapman* that convicts and sailors were not allowed to venture, another vital act of housekeeping was taking place. The hierarchy of the ship's command needed to develop their narrative of the events that brought about the shooting and subsequent massacre. They already had the convict Michael Collins in protective custody, having shared his tale of a planned convict mutiny during the previous days. The problem was that the word of Collins alone would not be enough to convince the receiving authorities in Sydney.

Surgeon Dewar sent word to the prison. A thirty-one-year-old labourer, John Ryan, originally from Cork, was to be brought to the cuddy. Michael Collins and the surgeon were waiting and when the guards escorted Ryan into the room, Dewar went out, leaving the two convicts alone. Ryan later claimed he had no idea why he was standing before Collins, a man who had betrayed his fellow convicts. The reason became clear in an instant. Collins did not delay. He implored John Ryan to give evidence to Dewar naming four convicts who were to become captain, officer, doctor, and mate once the official holders of those offices were murdered in the now aborted mutiny. He wanted him to give the same evidence that he himself had given the officers. In doing so, Ryan would corroborate and ultimately strengthen the story of the mutiny and go some way towards justifying the calamity of the night before. Ryan was chosen for this, claimed Collins, because they were fellow county-men. These sub-cultures of solidarity were commonplace not only on convict ships but in prisons in Ireland and Britain.

After a short silence passed between the two men, Surgeon Dewar returned to the cuddy. A climate of menace prevailed on the ship because the killings had just happened a matter of hours earlier. A terrible reali-sation dawned on John Ryan and he knew that he was in a perilous situation. Standing in the cuddy between a treacherous fellow convict and a senior officer whom he knew was capable of allowing extreme brutality, there was little room for manoeuvre. In that moment he decided to call on the only weapon in his armoury. He fell to his knees in front of Dewar declaring, 'I know nothing about this any more than a child unborn.'

'You damned rascal,' replied Dewar. 'If you don't give the same evi-dence as Collins has done you shall be flogged until near dead and shot afterwards.' The surgeon did not roar or scream in the same way as Baxter might have done but there was no mistaking the tone and seriousness of his threat.

'Sir, I have nothing to tell you unless I tell you lies.' Ryan looked on in despair as Dewar suddenly left the room, leaving him alone again with Collins. A moment later Captain Drake appeared. Ryan again fell to his knees and repeated the same lament about his ignorance to any mutiny. Drake repeated the threat just made by Dewar. He went out of the cuddy and both men immediately returned together to confront Ryan.

'If you give the same information as Collins. If you name the same prisoners as he has done then you will have plenty of money in your pocket. You will be given so much a year from the owners of this ship. It will save the men's lives and you shall go home again.' The Cork native reflected for some time and made a decision.

John Ryan chose to confess that he did know the names of the four men selected to fill the main officer positions once the convicts had taken the ship. He corroborated the story given by Michael Collins, arguing later that he did so to save the lives of the men in the prison. It is not known whether he received the promised financial inducements but given the events that followed at the end of the voyage, this is unlikely. Interestingly, Ryan felt that Dewar and Drake believed he was 'a good man' and that they disbelieved his support of the Collins story. Adding confusion to this whole scenario, in later testimony he took the blame for coercing his corroboration away from the two officers and placed it firmly on Collins.

To add to this perplexing account was the testimony of Lieutenant Christopher Busteed. He later claimed that Surgeon Dewar was most fair and reasonable in his interrogation of John Ryan, making no threats of flogging, hanging or shooting. While he did believe the evidence given by the two convicts, he felt that the possibility of a successful mutiny was very slim under the circumstances. The prisoners did not have the means to effect such a daring plan. At the time, however, he did believe there was a conspiracy at work but in hindsight he had revised his opinion on this. In Busteed's opinion, any and all cruel treatment and indignities aimed at the convicts from that moment forward were the result of the testimony of Collins and Ryan. This was also the point at which he noticed a deterioration in the attitude of Third Mate Baxter and many of the sailors towards the prisoners. The poison of suspicion, whatever the source, was now infecting everybody on the vessel and there was no cure.

The journey continues; so do the punishments
In the aftermath of the shooting a new calm settled across the decks of the *Chapman*, but it was a somewhat uncertain existence faced by the officers, soldiers, prisoners and sailors. Nobody was immune from the consequences of what had happened. The most troubling outcome for the convicts was the fear of the night and the dangers posed by an

unruly and panic-stricken regiment of soldiers. For up to ten days after the shooting the smallest noise coming from the prison during the night was seen by the soldiers as a signal and was duly punished. In the crowded and muggy atmosphere of the wooden prison the convicts were not even permitted to cough for fear it would trigger alarm amongst the soldiers.

It was Baxter's decision to punish the men for coughing. He decided that this was a signal, a form of non-verbal communication between the convicts that only they would understand. He called these noises 'insinuating coughs' and, because of the air quality in the prison and the general health of the men, numerous punishments were administered for this 'crime'. Likewise, the prisoners were not permitted to rattle their chains in any way lest they be seen as trying to signal to each other. If a prisoner made any noise with his chains, or muffled them with his handkerchief in order to prevent rattling, he was flogged. One account claimed that only about twenty men escaped punishment during this phase. The prisoners were placed in an impossible and unpredictable situation where they were in constant fear that the slightest vibration or thud would be misconstrued and lead to flogging or another escalation.

Perhaps most perplexing was the behaviour of the soldiers. They effectively surrendered to their most extreme nightmares and existed in a state of permanent unwarranted terror. An inquiry later found that they were as much in fear of the convicts as if it was they themselves shackled in the prison at their mercy. A sense of indifference fell upon Baxter who, ironically, was probably the source of the perpetual anxiety that was taking hold of the soldiers. Their reaction was all the more puzzling given that they were the ones with easy access to firearms. They were the ones with the legal authority to use those weapons. They were the ones on the other side of heavily chained prison doors. Surgeon Dewar claimed that part of the fear came from the fact that two of the sailors, Nelson and Crawley, were accused of being part of the conspiracy. The wider team of soldiers and sailors were fearful that the corruption may not end there, that there may be other silent conspirators at work among their own ranks.

Knives, forks and any other potentially harmful utensil was removed from the reach of the convicts. Any man found in possession of such offensive material was rewarded with punishment. It was later claimed that during this period convicts were concealing these items for each other, thus giving further justification for fear and over-reaction among the soldiers. The convicts implored Dewar to run an additional chain cable through the prison, further securing the occupants, but he refused on the grounds that this would endanger their health. Instead he implored them to ensure that such an additional security measure would not be necessary.

By 20 April the post-shooting routine had taken hold and it was very different from those monotonous weeks that marked the first month at sea. One further point of intolerance for the officers was the issue of broken irons and any man found to have defective shackles was punished. On that day alone, a full forty-six men were punished for having damaged irons. This may have been the bloodiest day of the voyage. On that same day many bloodstained items belonging to the dead and wounded were tossed overboard and the decks were again thoroughly scrubbed. The wounded convicts were reported to be doing well with no addition to the sick list. Conditions at sea remained calm, if not on the ship.

The convicts continue to fall

Seven months earlier, in September 1816, Thomas Mulholland was arrested while drinking porter in a public house in Cook Street in Dublin. The thirty-one-year-old was accused of being part of a gang of highway robbers menacing long-distance travellers on the roads into and out of the city. Two nights earlier a blacksmith named John Kelly was attacked while making his way home through Donnybrook. Although he put up a fierce resistance to his four assailants, Kelly eventually succumbed to their aggression. As well as money, the men relieved their quarry of a gold watch on a chain, seeds, a key, a lancet and a knife. When they were arrested the next day, the watch was found in Mulholland's possession.[84] Sentenced to death but commuted to transportation on board the *Chapman*, this would be Thomas Mulholland's final criminal act. At approximately 5 p.m. on 21 April the following year he died quite suddenly and unexpectedly at sea as a result of gunshot wounds sustained a few nights earlier on his journey to New South Wales. Forty minutes later his body was 'committed to the deep' in a traditional burial at sea.

His unexpected death did not interrupt the business of the ship, how-ever, and the punishments continued. By the end of that same day no fewer than thirty-four convicts were flogged for various misdemeanours, mostly related to the condition of their irons.

In the midst of all of the punishment and death, Surgeon Dewar decided that from this day forward, on a daily basis, the convicts and all the crew should each be served half an ounce of lime juice and half an ounce of sugar. Lime juice was by this time a well-practised nautical remedy for the treatment and cure of scurvy. With the threat of infection now greatly increased due to the occurrences of death and bleeding on board the ship, Dewar could no longer afford to take any chances. At any rate, a fresh consignment of fruit was taken on board at Porto Praya, including limes.

Despite the relevant calm that was restored to the ship, the conse-quences of the shooting were still at play during the following week. On 23 April, James Roberts, a fifty-year-old Limerick man transported for the offence of 'coining', died suddenly from gunshot wounds. His body was quickly despatched to the sea and the punishments continued on the ship. Thirty-year-old James McGrady from Kilkenny, convicted of burglary and felony, was given seventeen lashes. Convicted of sheep steal-ing, Matthew Daw was thirty-eight and from Galway. He was punished with eighteen lashes. Finally for that day, twenty-four-year-old John McDonough from Kerry – also an animal thief – was given eighteen lashes. The men were all deemed to have committed the same offence of muffling their irons in order to prevent them from making noise.

Post-voyage testimony from several convicts claimed that the rate of punishments for seemingly innocuous actions was greatly accelerated after the 17 April shootings. This was supported by written evidence in the journals of both Drake and Dewar. The screams of four men were heard across the decks on 24 April as the floggings persisted. Thomas Higgins was nineteen years old and found himself on the *Chapman* because he stole two silver teaspoons and one silver salt spoon from the home of James Warren in Sackville Street, Dublin. For some unspeci-fied offence he now endured twelve lashes on the back on the orders of Surgeon Dewar. The twenty-six-year-old pickpocket James Talbot, mentioned earlier, was given twelve lashes for insolence to the captain of the deck. He allegedly implied that the prisoners were not yet finished with their plot. Christopher Kelly was convicted of vagrancy at Dublin City Sessions in July 1816. His crime was somewhat more serious than suggested because Kelly had been sighted on several occasions follow-ing a number of 'well-dressed females' through Dame Street. In fact, his behaviour was so distressing to the victims that it necessitated their taking shelter inside a shop.[85] He was witnessed acting in an identical manner in Sackville Street. Now, many months later on the *Chapman*, he was administered twelve lashes on his back for 'making water' on the deck. In another part of the official record this offence was referred to as 'uncleanliness'. John Hay, a twenty-four-year-old pickpocket from Sligo, suffered twelve lashes for insolence.

The next prisoner to die on the *Chapman* was thirty-six-year-old Daniel Parker. In October 1815 he was convicted of horse stealing at Dublin City Sessions and sentenced to death. This was commuted to transportation but Parker's life and sentence ended prematurely at sea on 25 April 1817, again as a result of gunshot wounds sustained a week ear-lier. At this stage, with so many convicts now dead, either as an immediate or delayed result of the shooting of 17 April, the voyage was now turning into a disaster for Drake and Dewar. Instead of easing up on the punish-ments, however, they remained strongly committed to the near torture of their healthy convicts, and for the slightest of reasons.

Thomas Hall was the next man punished. In June of the previous year he connived his way into the home of John Gayner at Aungier Street in Dublin on the pretence of clearing the gutters. While the already suspi-cious servant, Bridget Dobbin, went to fetch a broom and box, Hall got to work. Dobbin apprehended the would-be gutter cleaner making his way outside carrying a bundle in his arms. Without waiting for an explanation, she lifted up his coat and spotted a pair of her master's panta-loons, as well as several other items. As Hall attempted to run the woman shouted 'Stop thief!' and two male passers-by apprehended the forty-eight-year-old. When searched later he was found wearing a new black coat – put on in the house *during* the crime – as well as the pantaloons and a pair of breeches. Two other witnesses testified that Thomas Hall had also stolen from them in the previous weeks.[86] He now stood on the *Chapman* where he received twenty-four painful lashes. His crime?

He rattled his chains in the night. That same day, John Dooley, an animal thief from King's County, was also given twenty-four lashes for the same offence. It appeared that the possibility that chains may have been rattled innocently in a sleeping state was not entertained on the *Chapman*, particularly after 17 April.

Not many convicts on this voyage were decorated with a criminal moniker by a national newspaper but the activities of eighteen-year-old Joseph Morton caused a minor stir in the world of bookselling in August 1816 in Dublin. Labelled 'the literary swindler' by the *Freeman's Journal*, Morton presented himself at the premises of a bookseller named Samuel Jones in Trinity Street. He claimed to represent a Mr Mulvey who was staying at the Rock Hotel. The mysterious and ultimately non-existent Mr Mulvey apparently needed three dozen spelling books, two dozen copies of Sellon's *Abridgement* (a religious text) and four copies of Gough's *Arithmetic*. Somehow Morton persuaded Samuel Jones to willingly part with the books. When the transaction was discovered as a crime it received attention from the newspapers and Morton was subsequently apprehended by the Usher's Quay police division. Samuel Jones was apparently not his only victim.[87] Morton was clearly an audacious confidence trickster and like the others he stood on the decks of the *Chapman* in the early months of a seven-year sentence of transportation. Accused of attempting to break free from his chain, he too was punished alongside Hall and Dooley, with twenty-four lashes.

Although the daily floggings were likely designed to have the effect of creating a more compliant and timid body of prisoners, they did nothing to quell the sense of foreboding that was once again taking hold on the ship. On 27 April, ten full days after the shooting, the unfortunate William Leo was flogged once again. This time he was given four lashes on the back for insolence to the corporal of the guard. A fellow convict, John McArdle, was given twelve lashes for rattling his chains during the night. Investigators later found that this was another highly sensitive period on the ship. The slightest tap of a foot against timber would have raised the entire regiment of soldiers and the crew in defence against a perceived threat. This was exactly what happened at 9 p.m. on the night of 27 April, when the rattling of chains was heard from within the prison. The soldiers and crew believed the prisoners were attempting to rise and so took up arms. Following a short investigation, the alarm was called off and the officers were satisfied that the noise was merely the result of some of the convicts getting out of bed too quickly without due care for the sound of their chains. The danger had passed but once again the *Chapman* was something akin to a floating barrel of gunpowder waiting for that crucial spark to detonate the explosion.

The second firing

The weather was warm and the progress steady on 28 April. The calm waters and relaxed exterior would have deceived the closest scrutiny. During the morning one of the convicts, Bryan Kelly, sent for Surgeon Dewar. Kelly was convicted of having forged notes and was on his way to begin a fourteen-year sentence of transportation. He reported that eight or nine days earlier one of his fellow prisoners, Patrick McCusker, began swearing the men in his mess into some sort of conspiracy. Armagh-born McCusker was forty-five years old and serving a sentence for committing a felony. Once more the intention was to take the ship but the prisoners were to fight until they were the only ten men left. Kelly further alleged that McCusker was concealing an iron bar, a large knife and two files, all in preparation for a break-out from the prison. He made his pronouncements to Dewar in front of several soldiers. In the afternoon Dewar sent for McCusker and ordered he be flogged with twenty-four lashes and confined to the poop deck.

News of this punishment undoubtedly spread throughout the ship as the afternoon gave way to evening. The reason for the punishment will also have spread among the soldiers and crew, heightening their levels of hostility towards the convicts to a greater extent than ever. The prisoners would have heard about the predicament of McCusker, now detained on the poop deck. Floggings were now a daily occurrence and no prisoner knew when he would be next. Ill-feeling was in plentiful supply when James Clements, one of the sentinels, reported that he heard a plot being discussed among the convicts at around 7.30 p.m. He alleged that they had devised a strategy for half of the convicts to take the front hatchway while the remainder took the sickbay and 'after-bulk head into the guard room'.

Everything remained quiet for a further hour. Inside the prison Terence Kiernan was settling down for the night. According to his account, all of the convicts were in their beds. From his position he claimed he could hear Third Mate Baxter outside plotting with Clements. Baxter allegedly pressed Clements that it was time to move forward with an attack on the prison. The junior officer argued that it was too soon but the third mate pointed out that this was the best time because the officers had all retired to their cabins for the evening. 'We shall have longer time to play at them,' Baxter is alleged to have professed gleefully. With that the second shooting began.

'Fire away my brave boys. Don't be commanded by captain, officers or superintendent and I will be accountable for it.' Kiernan painted a dramatic picture of a soon-to-be triumphant swashbuckling general sweeping his army into a final victorious battle. The reality was that soldiers were stationed at various cramped locations on the exterior perimeter of the prison and the best they could hope for was a few well-placed shots in the dark.

Surgeon Dewar was sitting in the cuddy with Lieutenant Busteed and the captain's brother Richard when he heard the first shot. On rushing out on deck he claims to have heard Captain Drake shouting 'avast firing'. He claimed that he, Busteed, Richard, Captain Drake and the other officers all pressed very hard to stop the soldiers firing. It stopped after about fifteen minutes but not before a shot passed very close to Dewar's head. Both the captain and his brother later claimed to Dewar that in the midst of the mayhem they heard some of the soldiers shout out 'shoot the bloody doctor'. The captain advised his surgeon to take caution while moving about the deck at night from that time onwards.

The doctor's mate, convict Patrick Smith, was asleep inside the hospital when the shooting began. He testified that it was the shot and not any forward rushing of the convicts that woke him. He believed the men were all in bed and perfectly quiet. Calculations on the length of the shooting varied wildly from between two to fifteen minutes, ironically with the officers of the ship claiming the longer estimate. In fact, the officer of the guard claimed it was a full half-hour. The convict James Talbot claimed that somewhere between twelve and twenty shots were fired while William Leo estimated five or six. The soldiers claimed that the shooting began as a result of the sound of a rush of prisoners about an hour after Clements allegedly heard them plotting.

One factor that remained undisputed by all was the central role once again of Third Mate James Miles Baxter. From his position on the other side of the timber wall he came to the fore scuttle quite close to where Terence Kiernan was in his bed. Instead of using a musket he pushed through with a pistol and ordered the soldiers to do the same. 'Fire in this way,' he ordered, 'and then you will weed them. Leave off firing with your muskets, it is of no use firing with them. Fire with our own pistols in this way.' Some of the soldiers duly obeyed their senior officer and several shots were fired in the manner that he ordered. This evidence would support the notion that Baxter was partly responsible for working the crew and soldiers into a frenzied hatred of the convicts. Captain Drake later claimed that when he ordered the soldiers to stop shooting and the gunner to cease distributing weapons to the crew, his commands fell on deaf ears. He described their collective demeanour as 'exasperated' and being in a high state of insubordination. When the shooting and the pleas for mercy died down it was time once again to assess the damage. Even though the incident ended much quicker than that of ten days earlier, there was no doubt that blood was once again flowing on the prison deck of the *Chapman*.

The prison becomes a mortuary again

The shooting took place at approximately 8.30 p.m., and at 10 p.m. some of the senior officers accompanied by a guard of soldiers entered the prison. A subsequent investigation attempted to understand why they felt it safe to venture in on that night but not immediately following the previous shooting. It was eventually explained away by the existence of different degrees of terror on both nights, with less of a threat felt following the second shooting. None of the official records stated exactly who entered the prison on the night of 28 April but it can be assumed that Drake, Dewar, Baxter and possibly Busteed were among the party.

The casualty number was not as high as the first shooting but, nonetheless, still horrific. Armagh native John McArdell, punished with twelve lashes just the previous day, died within the first four or five minutes of the shooting according to his mess-mate, Terence Kiernan. Four or five other men lay wounded as a result of the gunfire. The injured were removed to the sickbay, where they were received by Doctor's Mate Patrick Smith. Kiernan could not later remember whether the dead man was removed from the prison that night.

Another convict lost his life during the chaos of that night, but not inside the prison. William Leo later testified how there were twelve convicts confined to the poop deck for various misdemeanours. He claimed that the soldiers were ordered to 'cut us to pieces' should a firing start in the main prison below. The previous night, during the false alarm, it appeared that this may become reality when one of the sentries attempted to cut Leo. He raised his arm to protect his face and received cuts to the elbow and wrist. At that point a sergeant appeared to announce the false alarm and so Leo escaped with his life once more. When the shooting ended on the night of 28 April, Baxter emerged before the prisoners on the poop deck. When asked by the sentry what he wanted, the agitated third mate replied, 'I want to kill one of those rascals.' He ran to a weapons storage box and returned with what Leo believed was a blunderbuss. What happened next was unclear but one shot was fired and the blood of the convict Bryan Kelly splattered across the deck. The twenty-eight-year-old forger from Dublin, whose evidence earlier that day had quite likely contributed so much to the night's events, now lay dead on the poop deck.

William Leo and the remaining ten living convicts did not move or make a sound for fear that one of them may be next in the firing line. For the remainder of the night Bryan Kelly's body was left in the spot where it fell. The following morning First Mate Millbank arrived and ordered the body to be wrapped in a tarpaulin and removed. Baxter removed the chains from the corpse. He was heard denying that it was he who killed Kelly. Surgeon Dewar later testified that he heard the fatal shot was fired by John Jordan, one of the soldiers. The first investigation following the voyage was unable to make a conclusion on the killing of Bryan Kelly. It was merely declared that 'such facts appeared with regard to his death, so distinguishable in incident and apparent principle from the other cases of fatality occurring at the time of the general firings during the voyage, as to have led to the commitment of a party for trial.' Judgement on the shooting of Bryan Kelly was essentially left to another court to decide. His killing was ultimately more problematic because of its cold-blooded nature. While the men in the prison were shot under the guise of being about to mutiny or storm the doors, the same could not be said for the poop deck, where twelve chained men hardly posed a similar threat.

★

As the *Chapman* continued on the journey to New South Wales amidst the anarchy of that night, the ramifications of two separate shooting events ten days apart were too strong not to seal a horrific fate for the remaining convicts. To add to the drama, John McArdell and Bryan Kelly were the only convicts to be shot dead in the second incident but they were not the only ones to die on the ship that day. Thirty-five-year-old Longford murderer Oliver Wallace also lost his life that day. He died as a result of wounds sustained during the shooting on 17 April. As the death toll continued to rise, the fatalities now spanned two shootings. The 'entire ship's' company – officers, seamen and troops – were by then gripped by an insane dread of the convicts.'[88] Despite the shooting, the flogging and the loss of life, the stage was set for what was probably going to be the most extremely brutal part of the voyage. Lockdown.

4

Shockwaves at Sea

By the end of April 1817, the die was cast. The fate of the surviving convicts on the *Chapman* was sealed. The repeated armed confrontation of allegedly mutinous convicts by an out-of-control crew and guard meant that there would be no return to the peaceful monotony of the early weeks of the voyage. The death toll was rising and the ships' hospital was surely running out of space for the wounded. According to one of his own officers, the captain was seldom sober, particularly in the evenings when the ship was most likely to be confronted by danger. The events of the night of 28 April pushed the lived experience on the ship across the line towards a number of irreversible consequences. What little freedom the convicts enjoyed was now over. Life on the remainder of the voyage would include the almost daily spilling of the blood of impoverished and famished Irish convicts. The killing had not ended, but at least the sailors and prisoners would not have to endure another large-scale armed stand-off. Despite the fact that the journey was not yet halfway through, there was a surreal notion that it was now in its concluding phase. This phase would be dominated by the consequences of those two bloody nights.

Chaining them up
It was not easy to forget that the *Chapman* and all the other convict transports were essentially floating prisons and were subject to the same

mechanics of control and confinement as places of detention on land. In land-based prisons the convict was subjected to almost round-the-clock surveillance and penal reformers from John Howard and Elizabeth Fry to Jeremy Bentham all sought to improve living conditions while at the same time retaining the trappings of incarceration. On a convict ship it was not necessarily possible to observe the convicts at all times unless armed guards were placed inside the prison. It was necessary, therefore, to implement strategies where the gaolers (captain and crew) could be somewhat assured of the security of their convict cargo without have eyes on them at all times. On the *Chapman* the dynamics of surveillance roared to the top of the priority list for the officers after 28 April. The problem for Drake and Dewar was that their ocean-bound prison had limited capacity for meeting what were perceived to be heightened security threats. It became necessary to utilise and enhance existing techniques.

One of the most basic and common methods used was that of 'ironing', where handcuffs were applied, sometimes with leg irons. Some convicts were placed in irons for a portion of their time on the ship, others for the entire duration. This was typically reflected by the demeanour of the captain or surgeon.[89] The early conduct of the convicts will, of course, have played a role. The spectre of chains loomed large over the convict body on the *Chapman* to the extent that it can be safely assumed that all the prisoners were shackled in this way during the night-time in the prison and quite possibly during much of the day. During the more tranquil early month and a half of the voyage some use was made of the chain cable method of restraining the prisoners. This was a system whereby a chain was run around the prison attached to certain potentially noncompliant individuals. The chain cable remained a common presence as an extra layer of restraint during the remainder of the transportation period. Following the shooting of 28 April, it became the first line of defence on a ship that Captain Drake believed needed defending.

Surgeon Dewar would later employ a somewhat curious and roundabout defence of his liberal use of the chain cable from the beginning of May onwards. He claimed that the convicts became so agitated by the 'dreadfully exasperated and so irritable' state of the crew and soldiers that they themselves beseeched him to extend the cable.[90] In fact, it emerged later that the prisoners made this request prior to the 28 April shooting but Dewar, as we have seen, resisted on the grounds that it would imperil their general health. Rather than increasing the measure as a means of restraining the convicts, he claimed it was a way to protect them from a nervous crew and guard, who would in turn be eased by this further layer of security. He saw it as a means of guarding against further 'dreadful consequences which were to be apprehended from the disposition of the soldiers and crew'.[91] Dewar's decision was supported by a later investigation, which decried the 'hair-trigger terror of the ship's company'.[92]

On the night of 30 April, Dewar ordered that fifty-four convicts be confined on the chain cable as it was passed through the prison. How these men were selected is not known but it is likely that Third Mate Baxter and some of his lieutenants will have had influence over the decision-making process. The next day, from 4 p.m. onwards, the number on the cable increased to seventy-three. This number held steady for much of the month of May and for the most part the selected men were not shackled until late afternoon or evening. This did, of course, ensure a long night in the prison, confined to the same space, unable to walk around, dependent on the position of those chained on either side. This will have also further compromised the hygiene of the prison and health of the men, who would have been unable to safely use any toilet facilities that were available. By 25 May the numbers on the chain cable increased to 101, meaning that more than half the surviving convicts were now chained together in the prison for significant portions of the twenty-four-hour day. Figures were not recorded on a daily basis for June and July but it was later noted that the number confined in this way at one point rose to 106.

Retribution

The second grave consequence following the late-April shooting was an onslaught of near-daily corporal punishment of the convicts. The suspicion and anger toward them was so bad that when they were brought out on deck for regular punishment or even wine rations they were subjected to random blows from the soldiers and sailors. The officers claimed that this behaviour took place without their consent and against their orders. There is no evidence that this behaviour was common during the first six weeks of the voyage. One convict suggested that the crew and soldiers brought buckets to the prison on several nights during May with a view to smothering everyone inside. This account was not given much credence by investigators and was not supported by any other convicts, neither was it made clear how the buckets would be weaponised for this purpose.

We have already seen how *Chapman* prisoners were severely punished between 17 and 28 April, but the worst was yet to come. The most common type of corporal punishment on convict ships was flogging using the cat-o'-nine-tails. It was at its most prevalent during the eighteenth and early nineteenth centuries, with a declining use after 1820. According to O'Toole, the average flogging ranged between six and twenty-four lashes.[93] Flogging was used in the penal system at this time not only as a punishment but as a means of making the recipient a better member of society.[94] On this journey it became clear that it was used for neither punishment nor reform but only for the purposes of cruelty and retribution.

The volume of floggings stepped up in earnest from early May onwards. Francis Murphy, the convicted thief who was already well established as an enemy of the officers, was brought up on deck at 4 p.m. on the afternoon of 2 May, where he was given twenty-four lashes on the back for 'having in his possession an instrument for the purpose of taking off the close prisoners' handcuffs and wishing Peter Allan to make use of it in that way'.[95] That same day, Patrick McKenna, a robber from Antrim, was given eighteen lashes for allegedly stating that if the convicts did not take the ship in fine weather then they would take it in bad weather. Investigators later queried the context of this statement and who had heard it, but it is not clear if an answer was forthcoming from Dewar.

Sometimes the surgeon noted who was punished and why. On other occasions he merely noted that a flogging had taken place without providing further details. A forty-six-year-old animal thief named John Dooley, from King's County, was brought on deck on 4 May and flogged for uncleanliness. Again, the surgeon was queried as to the nature of the uncleanliness and how it was allowed to happen. No response was recorded. At 8.30 p.m. that night, Martin Dungannon was given twenty-four lashes for muffling his irons.[96] This was an ongoing conundrum for the convicts. If they made a noise while chained in the prison, particularly at night, they were flogged. Yet, if they tried to silence their chains by using items of clothing then this was viewed with suspicion and they were flogged.

The following day the surgeon ordered no fewer than 104 lashes on the bodies of seven convicts. It was the most brutal day seen on the ship yet and one that was marked by the screams of bloodied and tormented convicts. The carnage began at 8 a.m., when the aforementioned Patrick McKenna was served with a further twelve lashes for being out of bed and rattling his chains at an 'improper hour'. Thomas Marlow was a twenty-seven-year-old servant from Westmeath and in March 1816 he was brought before a magistrate in Dublin for stealing a number of silver coins from his master, Ralph Shaw of White's Lane.[97] Like many others, Marlow found himself on the *Chapman* for wholly non-violent crimes and now he was brutalised alongside McKenna at the same hour, and also with twelve lashes.

Three hours later brought a mass flogging of a further five convicts. Thomas Kenna was given twelve lashes on the back and twelve 'on the breech'.[98] Patrick Ward, a twenty-eight-year-old labourer from Meath, was given twelve lashes on the back. Forty-year-old James Johnson from Roscommon was given twenty-one lashes on the back. John Flynn, a thirty-year-old Dubliner, was given twelve on the back. Finally, the unfortunate and now recurrently punished William Leo was given twelve lashes. These five men were flogged for suspicious conduct. Drake revealed that the officers had that day received a list of nineteen names of conspirators related to the second shooting. Whether or not these five men were part of that list is not known, although it can be assumed William Leo was included. Whether justified or not, Leo was firmly and permanently in the crosshairs of the officers, who appeared to be looking for any reason to punish him.

During the following week the floggings were sporadic, with just one or two recorded per day. The brutality seen on 5 May was surpassed eleven days later when fifteen prisoners were flogged. While the decision to formally punish a convict was in the gift of the surgeon-superintendent, it is not clear to what extent Dewar was influenced or even overruled by others in the officer class such as Drake or Baxter.

Cornelius Connor was thirty years old and one of a family of four prisoners from Cork on the *Chapman* for animal theft. He received the first punishment of the day for calling Third Mate Baxter a 'damned rogue'. Sixty-one-year-old horse thief Patrick Finnegan from Louth was next to be punished, for uncleanliness. A further twelve unnamed convicts were flogged for 'having in their berth a lever and piece of iron hoop'.[99] John McKenna, aged nineteen and also from Louth, was flogged for having a piece of tin in the shape of a knife.

The mass floggings continued at the end of May and at regular intervals during June and July.[100] On 31 May thirteen convicts were punished. Thomas Marlow was given a further thirty-six lashes; William Roddy twenty-four; Thomas McGiff thirty-six; Martin Dungannon thirty-six; Andrew McMahon twenty-four and John Dooley twenty-four. Their alleged crime was 'cutting the main deck in the prison'.[101] A further seven unnamed men were flogged for different charges. On 3 June another seven men were punished, one of whom was twenty-three-year-old George McMullin, who committed the offence of laughing. The others were William Walsh, Andrew Murtagh, Michael Leonard, Andrew McMahon, John King (on suspicion of a further conspiracy), and John Gilshenon [*sic*]. It was now becoming clear that the officers were selecting some convicts for flogging on a regular basis. It was likely that old grudges remained and suspicions were aroused among the crew and soldiers towards certain prisoners. Punishments were doled out at will and for the slightest misdemeanour. It was important to remind the prisoners who was in control.

On 8 June another six men were flogged for varying unwritten crimes. James Finn, John Dooley (again), Christopher Quinn, Charles Darley and John Ennis, who was apprehended by the nightwatchman in Bishop Street. Five days later and another four men were flogged. A burglar named Andrew McMahon from Clare was punished for making a noise and fighting. Michael McDonagh was disciplined for making a noise with his chains during the night. Pat Reilly and James Hayes, the latter from Kildare, were flogged for fighting. Drake was later queried in writing by his superiors as to why there was any presumption of a conspiracy among the convicts given these incidences of infighting in the prison. This is one of the few recorded examples of fighting among the convicts themselves, with the likelihood that geographically-based subcultures of solidarity existed in the prison, thus making it an almost self-governing community.

The next mass punishment was noted on 17 June, when five men were flogged. Patrick Mahony was a twenty-four-year-old robber from Cork whose misfortune was to make noise at night against the orders of the ship. Patrick Leydon, also twenty-four and from Tipperary, was punished for the same offence. Michael Flynn, Michael Peters and (again) John Gilshenon [*sic*] were all flogged for neglect and insolence. Four days later six prisoners were punished for variously making noise, uncleanliness and insolence. As June turned into July this pattern continued and the slightest infringement had the effect of causing a flogging. While Baxter and his subordinates were responsible for the delivery of these penalties, it is worth remembering that it was Surgeon-Superintendent Dewar who gave the orders.

The final recorded floggings of the voyage took place on 10 July. Edward Jameson was a thirty-nine-year-old animal thief from Down, flogged for having a 'pick lock' in his possession. John Rowe and Thomas Higgins were guilty of making a noise, while Charles Connell suffered for 'heaving a pick lock into Jamieson's [*sic*] berth'.[102] The captain was later queried as to why Jameson would have been flogged if the offending item was thrown into his berth by another prisoner in the first place. Should there not have been a proper investigation that would possibly have proven Jameson's innocence and spared him twenty-four lashes? This incident is an example of the rash behaviour that now marked the officers of the *Chapman*.

The murder of Francis Lucy

The squabbles that divided the voyage tended to happen along traditional lines, convicts versus everyone else aboard not forced to make the journey. On the *Chapman*, however, the threat of some sort of eruption between the soldiers and sailors was never far away. The real peril lay in the possibility of some unexpected incendiary event causing a physical flare-up of the kind that allegedly took place on land at Porto Praya. Suspicion of the sailors grew as the voyage progressed and probably began with concerns over Nelson and Crawley in early April. The most serious incident to strike the soldier-sailor relationship came in the early hours of the morning of 25 May, after the officers had all gone to bed. It began at 10.30 p.m. the previous night when John Sandon, sentry on the cuddy, allegedly heard Crawley and the convict John Jackson plotting to cut Mr Millbank's throat that night and lamenting that they were not free to kill Surgeon Dewar. All remained calm for the next few hours. Chatter of this nature was probably not unusual and Nelson and Crawley were already believed to be firmly on the side of the prisoners by this time.

Crew members Nelson and Crawley were detained on the jolly boat along with another sailor, Francis Lucy, and one of the convicts, John Jackson. All four men were in chains. The jolly was a type of utility boat typically found on sailing ships during the eighteenth and nineteenth century. Among other things it was used for short journeys taking the occupants to and from a sailing ship that was moored in a harbour. It was also commonly used as a standby place of detention for miscreants during a voyage, particularly sailors who could not be put into the main prison on a convict transport. At about quarter past one in the morning, one of the soldiers on the poop deck, Jordan, shouted at the four men in the jolly boat to keep their heads down or they would be fired upon. Captain Drake was awakened in his cabin by the sound of gunfire. He ran out onto the deck in his nightwear, demanding to know what had happened. The sentinel on the poop deck shouted to him that the prisoners in the jolly boat were attempting to rise. Several convict and sailor eyewitnesses claimed that after making his threat to the occupants in the jolly boat, Jordan fired anyway. His shot struck Nelson in the leg. The next shot was fired by soldier James Clements and struck John Jackson, though not fatally. A third and fourth soldier also fired into the boat, where both Crawley and Lucy were wounded. There were an estimated eleven shots in all. At this point one of the soldiers, Hogan, appeared at the side of the boat in a somewhat frenzied state. 'Who is the damned rascal that has told lies of me,' he demanded. The men in the jolly indicated that it was Francis Lucy. With very little hesitation the soldier lifted his weapon, pointed it at the head of the wounded sailor, and pulled the trigger several times.

The impact of the gunfire caused the weapon to recoil from Hogan's hand and fall into the sea. Six different sailors described how the soldier had 'blown Lucy's brains out'. Soon after the killing the ever-present Third Mate Baxter appeared on the scene. Along with one of the sailors, Henry Jennings, he unceremoniously cast the body of Francis Lucy overboard. Nelson later recalled that the corpse was in a dreadful state 'and would have been a shocking spectacle in the daylight'. As the weather was so hot he claimed the unfortunate sailor's remains would have 'putrefied' by morning.[103] William Jones, an apprentice on the ship, described how 'the smell of Lucy's dead body was quite poisonous' by the time he was buried at sea.[104] Henry Jennings argued that 'the weather was so hot as we were not far from the line that if he had remained till morning on the boat, he would have been offensive'.[105]

Despite the horror of the scene, the three remaining men, Nelson, Crawley and the convict John Jackson, were left in the jolly boat with their wounds and the spray from those of the now-deceased sailor Francis Lucy for the remainder of the night. In keeping with their slapdash approach to every crisis that happened on the ship, just as Lieutenant Busteed and Dr Dewar arrived on the scene the shooting stopped; Drake returned to his cabin to dress himself. He was apparently unaware of the horror that had just unfolded whereby one of the soldiers had just shot a chained-up sailor point blank in the head at close range. Four days later, the twenty-six-year-old robber from Limerick, John Jackson, also died from the wounds he sustained from the unprovoked shooting that night. The death toll from gunfire was rising on the *Chapman* and the voyage was just about halfway through.

Rationing

Yet another long-term consequence of the disruption that marked the voyage during the month of April centred on the distribution of food rations to the prisoners. On 30 June, Surgeon Dewar wrote the following letter to Captain Drake:

> The Convicts, having represented to me that their provisions are not issued to them agreeable to the established proportions, and as I have reason to believe there is some foundation for the complaint, I have therefore to request that you will make immediate enquiry into the same, and have

the irregularity corrected; and further that you will be pleased to state to
me in writing the quantity of Beef and Pork now due to the Convicts,
occasioned by the mistake that has arisen in issuing their Provisions.[106]

As surgeon-superintendent it was Dewar's responsibility to make decisions on the portions allocated to everyone on board, obviously with
special attention given to the prisoners, who made up the largest collective group on the vessel. The daily delivery of these rations was the
ultimate responsibility of Drake as captain. During May and June, it
was obvious that something had gone wrong with this process and the
convicts were experiencing difficulties. On 1 July 1817, Captain Drake
wrote the following response to Dewar:

> In compliance with your request of yesterday, respecting the Provision
> which has been Issued to the Convicts, that they complained of Not
> having had their full allowance of Beef and Pork, I have endeavoured as
> much as possible to find out the truth of this, of which the following is
> the result. The Gunner, who has served the Provisions out to the Convicts
> since the 13th or 14th of April, and who at that time had directions to
> Serve it out according to Establish'd proportion given to him, informs
> me that in consequence of the irregular Weight of the Pieces of Beef and
> Pork, some Pieces weigh'd Ten Pound, others only Seven, instead of Eight;
> that he weighed out the full allowance, without regarding the Number
> of Pieces, and asserts that he has always given them their full weight; but
> further to find out the truth, I have compared the Quantity of Provisions
> broached with the Quantity Issued out, which if the Gunner informs
> me right, and I have no reason to doubt his honesty. I have directed in
> future that the Beef and Pork is to be Served out by the Pieces, taking
> it for granted that the Pieces weigh as Marked on the Cask, and as the
> diff'e appears to be much against the Convicts by not having had it by the
> Pieces, I will Issue the same to them at your pleasure.[107]

The significance of this line of communication became clear at the end
of the voyage, but it is possible that Dewar and Drake were protecting
themselves by establishing a formal paper trail. In evidence later, Drake
claimed that he directed the steward to distribute food to the prisoners

according to the orders of Dewar and the official guidance provided by the government. He claimed that he heard nothing about the convicts having issues with the food from 17 April up to the receipt of Dewar's letter on 30 June. 'How,' he asked, 'could I suppose that anything was going wrong?'[108] He refuted any charge that he could possibly have defrauded the convicts out of their allocated rations. That Drake and Dewar did not verbally communicate on these issues at the end of June is unlikely. The official narrative laid out in these letters would later be demolished when the ship docked in Sydney.

In truth, the two most senior officers admitted here that the prisoners were at least deprived of their full allocation of meat. In their defence, they alleged that the mistake took place because of difficulties in measuring the portions made available, but this was later rejected by government store officials in Sydney, who argued that the casks of meat were all clearly marked according to weight and if this was correctly and evenly divided out then the proper amount would have been used. This was allowing for mistakes here or there. The implication was clearly put forward that the prisoners were purposely denied their full allocation of meat 'at a time when they most required the strength of its nourishment'.[109]

Something not written in the journals, testimonies and letters of the surgeon and captain, but later accepted by an official investigation, was that the prisoners were severely rationed in the immediate aftermath of the 17 April shooting up to 1 July. It became obvious that someone on the ship made a decision that partially starving the convicts into compliance or submission would be an effective strategy in regaining control. The only shortcoming admitted to by ship's personnel was in relation to the meat. The various stewards tasked with distributing all food during the period in question claimed that they followed orders according to notices given to them and also placed in the hospital. They further claimed that Captain Drake devised these notices and was personally responsible for the instructions. Drake and Dewar strongly denied these allegations, possibly placing the blame back at the feet of the stewards. The prisoners, meanwhile, claimed that they did not dare complain of their ongoing starvation after 17 April, only plucking up the courage by the end of June when the period of greatest volatility had subsided.

The starvation claimed to have been experienced by the convicts was found to be real. The quality, cooking and manner of delivery were not given the proper care and attention that was required. This was accounted for by the 'general state of the ship', but no specific motive was ascribed to the decision to treat the convicts in this manner. Using somewhat vague language, the principal investigator into events on the ship, Judge Darcy Wentworth, implied that captain and surgeon were not actually to blame for the shortfalls in food rations. He also rejected the notion that they could not be approached by prisoners wishing to complain. This was borne out, he claimed, by the response to their complaint in late June, after which the situation was rectified. So who starved the prisoners?

One of Wentworth's co-investigators, Colonial Secretary J.T. Campbell, took a harsher line against the officers and crew. He declared:

> Whilst the with-holding most fraudulently from these Miserable Wretches His Majesty's bountiful Allowance of Rations, until they were One and All of them Nearly in a starving and expiring Condition, exhibits but too Clearly the *quo Animo*, by which those Three Officers were actuated, and fixes on each of them a proportionate share of Delinquency.[110]

In this case he was speaking of Captain Drake, Surgeon Dewar and Third Mate Baxter. The difference in opinion between Campbell and his colleague possibly lies in the fact that he was the first Sydney-based official to board the ship after it moored in Sydney. He witnessed the consequences of the starvation of the prisoners. Despite the gradual malnourishment of the convicts, Wentworth later applauded the fact that only two of those that died on the voyage lost their lives to non-violent causes. Some of the others would remain crippled for life.

Final weeks at sea

The killing of Francis Lucy in the early hours of 25 May appears to have been the final fatal shooting on the voyage but it was not the final death. The following day, thirty-one-year-old John Malone died from gunshot wounds. Malone was from Monaghan and sentenced to death for housebreaking and robbery. The sentence was commuted to one of transportation but this turned out to be a temporary reprieve as he was caught in the crossfire of one of the April shootings into the prison on the *Chapman*. Three days later, fifty-seven-year-old James Collins from Cork passed away but the reasons were not recorded. Collins was convicted of sheep stealing, a crime that also earned him a death sentence that was commuted to transportation for life. The last recorded death on the ship came on 27 June, a full month before arrival in Sydney. Forty-one-year-old Christopher Kelly, a vagrant from Dublin – flogged in April for 'making water' on the deck – also died from causes not stated. While Kelly and Collins could both have been wounded in either of the April shootings, there could possibly have been a more likely explanation for their deaths. By the second half of May the convicts were forced to spend increasing lengths of time in the cramped, dirty and unventilated prison. This was a place where several men had already met their deaths and despite the best efforts of scrubbing and disinfecting there is no question that infection was a significant possibility.

At the end of convict and other voyages it was required that the surgeon provide a return outlining the medical state of his passengers. Dewar provided a tabulated report with the onboard personnel divided into 'convicts', 'guard' and 'seamen'. A total of seventy-one convicts were placed on the Sick List according to the figures. These included thirty-four for dysentery, three for pulmonic inflammation, three for fever and one each for stricture, syphilis and an amputated finger. Twenty-eight were listed as being cured of dysentery. An extraordinary twenty-eight convicts were reported on the sick list for gunshot wounds; eighteen were reported 'cured'. No guards or seamen reported sick with gunshot wounds.

Two convicts died on board during the voyage, while Dewar reported that seven lost their lives as a result of gunshots. Five convicts were 'killed' on board, presumably meaning that they lost their lives immediately during the different skirmishes. Two seamen also died in this manner. Three convicts ended the voyage on the sick list as a result of gunshot wounds but none were confined to bed. Eight convicts and one soldier were listed as 'fit objects for the hospital'.[111]

5

Aftershocks

After some 134 days at sea, the *Chapman* arrived at Sydney Cove on 27 July 1817. By contemporary standards it was an average journey length with no reports of any significant storms or technical difficulties to slow down the progress toward Australia. Without the benefit of their own words there really is no way to understand the emotions that the convicts experienced during the final hours as the ship approached the mooring point at Port Jackson. Writing of his journey into the port on board the *Hillsborough* in 1799, the convict William Noah described those final miles as not being marked 'by foreboding and dread but by joy and a sense of deliverance into a long and wished-for country'.[112] For him, New South Wales was once a place that suggested exile and punishment, a strange new land from which there was little or no promise of return. Now, after all those months at sea, it offered refuge from the starvation, cold, dirt, illness and death that marked the daily existence on the convict ship. As the *Chapman* moored in the harbour it was said to have looked like any other of the many convict transports that arrived during these years. To the casual onlooker there was nothing to suggest that the newly arrived vessel held such a broad swathe of unspeakable and horrific secrets. There was no outward expression of the volatile encounters that marked so much of the past four months and twelve days on this floating penal institution. With the arrival of the ship, the authorities on land began preparations for a well-established set of procedures that would see the human cargo delivered to onward destinations.

In the days after the ship landed in Port Jackson the residents of the colony were given a somewhat premature account of the floating tragedy that had just sailed into their midst. A local newspaper delayed publication to announce incorrectly that seven prisoners were killed on the ship that left Cork on 25 March. The report continued that they died during 'a daring mutiny' which was 'still more terrible' because the prisoners were joined in their escapade by a number of the crew.[113] A week later the same newspaper was unable to provide any further detail on the events that were so dramatically exposed after the arrival of the ship. It was likely a default stance of newspapers and those in officialdom to automatically blame convicts in any controversy where the facts were not yet fully established.

Although the prisoners of the *Chapman* were well aware that they had reached their destination, it is believed that they did not physically see the landscape with their own eyes for several days after arriving. In keeping with practices already instituted by the authorities in Sydney, almost all prisoners and crew remained on convict ships for several days after mooring. This was to allow for an in-depth health inspection and also an opportunity for prisoners to disclose any complaints they may have had about their treatment on the journey.[114] The convicts of the *Chapman* were forced to endure their nightmare for four further days and most accounts confirm that they remained chained in the prison during that waiting period. Traditionally, only convicts or crew requiring immediate hospitalisation were allowed onshore immediately. In keeping with the chaos that surrounded the voyage, three sailors – John Gill, George Speed and James Bigley – all deserted from the ship on the day it arrived.[115]

On 28 July, the day after their arrival, an order was drafted at Government House in Parramatta:

His Excellency the Governor directs John Thomas Campbell, Esquire, will be Pleased to proceed on board the Ship Chapman, Transport, recently arrived from Ireland, on Thursday next, the 31st instant, at 9 O'Clock in the Morning, for the purpose of Mustering and inspecting the Male Convicts arrived in that Ship, reporting their state and Condition in

Writing to His Excellency the Governor. Mr. Hutchinson, the Principal Superintendent, will attend Mr. Secretary Campbell to assist him in taking the Muster thus Ordered.[116]

This routine order signed by Major H.C. Antill was the opening salvo in a legal process that would see the preceding voyage of the *Chapman* subjected to numerous inquiries, investigations and criminal prosecutions. It would be more than a year and a half before the saga of this four-month nightmare voyage would be concluded and this part of the process gave rise to a whole new cast of characters.

John Thomas Campbell and the grisly truth

One of those determined to uncover the facts about the voyage was Colonial Secretary John Thomas Campbell. His function in government dictated that he would typically be the first to inspect a convict ship upon arrival. Born around 1770 to his mother Mary and father William, the vicar of Newry, John Thomas Campbell and his brothers were educated at home. During the early to mid-1790s he was part of the Bank of Ireland. The next historical traces find him in the Cape of Good Hope, again involved in some unspecified form of banking. While working there, Campbell was introduced to the visiting governor-designate of New South Wales, Lachlan Macquarie. He joined the Scottish-born official on his onward journey and they arrived in New South Wales on 1 January 1810. The two men formed a close bond and after arriving in the colony Macquarie appointed Campbell his secretary. It was a role Campbell relished and one that eventually morphed into the title 'colonial secretary'. John Thomas Campbell spent eleven years at Macquarie's side as his loyal friend, most trusted advisor and chief administrator. Together they oversaw a golden age of development in the colony, with the building of new infrastructure including public buildings and transport links along with more sophisticated layers of civic and social administration.[117] Campbell was a crucial ally of the progressive Governor Macquarie and appeared not only to influence his decisions but also to understand his ambitions for the colony. When Campbell boarded the *Chapman* for that routine inspection on the final day of July 1817, it could just as easily have been the governor himself. Ultimately, both men would be of a similar mind regarding what they encountered and, more importantly, they would formulate and support the same set of responses.

Campbell's involvement with the *Chapman* got off to an inauspicious start. He boarded the ship as planned at nine in the morning to oversee a muster of the convicts and a general inspection. The officers were well aware of his visit in advance, having been informed by letter the day after mooring. To Campbell's annoyance, Captain Drake was not on the ship when he arrived and did not return until an hour and a quarter after their appointed time. Campbell, accompanied by Superintendent of Prisoners Hutchinson, waited impatiently on the deck. It later transpired that Drake left the ship to go ashore shortly before Campbell was due to arrive. Campbell was appalled by Drake's behaviour and informed the captain that his rudeness was an affront both to himself and to the authority of the governor. Drake rejected this, claiming his conduct was not rude. He offered no apology. Campbell and Hutchinson had not yet met a single convict and already they had been disrespected by Drake.

Campbell later made it clear that he did not wish to begin the muster of the prison inmates until Captain Drake returned to his ship. Again in keeping with procedure, he wished him to witness and respond to any complaints that the prisoners may register against anyone in authority during the voyage. He also wished to hear the captain's account of any conduct, good or bad, on the part of the prisoners. By this time, he was anecdotally aware that there had been some sort of fracas during the passage from Ireland, but had no idea of the extent of the human destruction and mutilation.

The seed for the second point of disagreement between the parties was planted the day before Campbell boarded the ship. He had been informed by Superintendent Hutchinson that Drake was unwilling to release the convicts from their various chains and shackles until they were ready to be officially mustered in front of government inspectors before disembarkation. It was standard procedure that they be freed from their restraints once the ship moored in the destination port. The captain claimed he remained concerned about the safety of the ship and the potential indiscipline of the convicts, given all that had happened on the journey. In a letter to Drake on 30 July, Campbell generally accepted this decision but requested specifics. He asked the captain why he felt it necessary to ignore the usual regulations, what grounds he had for continuing to shackle the men, and what exactly was the security threat to the ship. Drake did not respond in writing and this immediately irked Campbell.

When the men finally came face-to-face on the deck of the *Chapman*, Campbell questioned Drake as to why he had not answered his questions from the previous day. The captain replied that from the tone of the Irishman's letter he believed him to be offended and so decided not to respond. Campbell asked the captain, this time to his face, specifically why the convicts remained in chains so many days after arrival. Drake responded insolently that he received the convicts in chains and would land them in chains. Campbell decided not to pursue this matter any further and instead asked Drake to produce the county or jail lists that should have accompanied the convicts on the voyage. Drake informed him that he received none. As these bureaucratic squabbles continued on deck, Campbell and Hutchinson could scarcely have predicted the horrors that awaited them when the prison doors were finally unlocked and the men brought forward for muster.

Seeing the light

When Mr. Secretary Campbell ordered Captain Drake to muster surviving convicts on deck, 160 gaunt, famished men, loaded with chains and bearing the marks of brutal floggings, staggered up from the foetid 'tween-decks prison.[118]

This is how that moment was described in an Australian newspaper 137 years after the event. Campbell's revulsion could not be disguised by the guarded and almost bureaucratic language he employed in his initial report on what he first encountered when the men emerged. His first declaration, having interviewed 176 of the surviving prisoners, was that no conspiracy or plot whatsoever existed. Two of those, Michael Collins and John Ryan, remained committed to their original allegations. Not surprisingly, he found that the prisoners were well treated until the night of the first shooting on 17 April. This is borne out by consistent convict evidence that they were shown little oppression up to this time.

Campbell's initial findings were certainly preliminary in that they would all be legally challenged later and so were not definitive. They were, however, based upon the immediate testimony he received from convicts, officers and crew. They must also have been shaped by the shock of some 170-plus emaciated and dazed prisoners stepping into the light for the first time in weeks. Describing their immediate fate following the hours after the shooting on 17 April, he explained how the 'miserable wretches in the prison', whether killed or wounded, spent the night lying naked or nearly naked on the prison floor. Some of them left their berth to cool down in the hot climate and oppressive and suffocating surroundings. He confirmed that the dead were not removed nor the wounded dressed until the following day. Campbell was the first figure in officialdom to express full sympathy for the suffering of the *Chapman* convicts. He reported to Macquarie that 'the sufferings and apprehensions of these poor creatures, cooped up as they were and fired on fore and aft, need not be commented on and can scarcely be exaggerated'.[119]

He was equally shocked by the extent of the punishment meted out for often very trivial wrongdoings. He noted that one convict in particular – he did not mention William Leo by name – was repeatedly flogged 'on the most frivolous, if not unjust charges'.[120] Between seventy-four and 100 men were chained naked to the iron cable, one group for a full twenty-four hours. Never fewer than seventy-four and sometimes as many as 106 were chained nightly in that same manner for most of the voyage after 17 April. He described a 'system of terror' that existed 'when these poor creatures were on the cable'. Should they 'express having a call of nature' they ran the risk of attracting the wrath of 'a brutal fellow, the 3rd Officer, called Baxter' who might beat, cut or shoot them. On the other hand, if they 'voided their excrement' where they lay then they ran the risk of being flogged for uncleanliness. He also noted the long-standing problem of convicts being barely able to move because their chains would make a noise. Making or concealing the noise of their chains was enough to earn a flogging.[121]

This initial investigation threw some further light on the starvation of the prisoners, particularly from 17 April onwards. After that first shooting the men were no longer given knives or any such implements to cut their meat. Some convicts broke the tin handles off their mugs to use for this purpose but any man that did so earned himself a flogging. This make-shift instrument was now seen by the officers and soldiers as a potential weapon. According to Campbell, many of 'these most unfortunate men were so tyrannized over that' they would have preferred to have been hanged for their original offence than subjected to the cruelties they endured. To further intensify their misery, they were denied a full half of their food allowance from the time of the first shooting until 10 or 11 July. In the words of the colonial secretary, 'they were nearly famished with hunger'.[122]

Revelations of the constant physical restraint of the convicts was another issue that attracted Campbell's disgust as the stories emerged from the first examination. He discovered that not once since leaving Cork over four months earlier were they allowed out of irons. He lamented that:

> Even those, who were lame of arms, lost as soldiers and sailors in fighting the battles of their country at Copenhagen and Waterloo, were thus starved, double ironed and chained to the iron cable. Many fainted from pure weakness on the cable, arising from hunger.[123]

He implored Macquarie to imagine a fellow human being in double irons, chained to a cable and handcuffed for all of three months, except for those times when he was released to be flogged. Such was the extent of the horror that Campbell felt he encountered at this stage, he referred his friend and superior to the official documents of the ship where punishments and restraints were formally recorded.

First judgement

Campbell's final summation of what should have been a somewhat standard inspection was damning. He declared that Captain Drake and his officers, Surgeon-Superintendent Dewar and many of the crew, were all guilty of 'inhuman, barbarous and cruel [conduct] beyond all reason, or what even mutiny itself, if the prisoners had been guilty of it, could have at all warranted'.[124] Ironically, he found Dewar – as a surgeon presumably – to 'have conducted himself very kindly and humanely'. As a superintendent, however, 'he seems to have lost sight of all compassion and of all judgement in adopting the false accusations of a couple of informers and of some of the ship's petty officers'.[125] He further discovered that when the convicts were searched for concealed weapons at various times, their clothes were taken up on deck, where their money was stolen. Several items of clothing were actually kept from them. Campbell did not apportion blame for this but the underlying suggestion appears to be that the officers and soldiers were willing to turn a blind eye to any such behaviour from the ordinary sailors. Perhaps this was a means of appeasing any mutinous inclinations on *their* part.

Campbell's devastating report came with a recommendation. He encouraged Macquarie to order a 'full investigation of these atrocious circumstances'. Evidence from the convicts themselves would be essential, he believed, in order to substantiate the charges that he believed were true. It was his final opinion that the conduct of the officers could not be justified and that they themselves should face appropriate punishment 'according to the overflowing measure of their cruelty and guilt'.[126] He attached a formal muster report to his letter, outlining in some greater detail the list of complaints levelled against the officers and soldiers.[127]

Campbell began his inspection of the *Chapman* on 31 July but the grim nature of his discoveries meant it continued into the following day. When he finally left the ship to write his report it is impossible to tell whether Drake or Dewar had any inclination of what was to follow. They did not have long to wait. On 2 August the colonial secretary sent a letter to Drake outlining the next steps. Campbell had put forward 'certain criminal charges' against the captain and his officers for their 'various frauds and a series of tyrannical conduct, oppressions and cruelty' toward the convicts from the moment the ship left Ireland.[128] The charges would be particularly focussed on the period from 17 April to 10 July and he hoped they would be met with suitable punishment. In his role as Secretary to the Government and a Magistrate of the Territory of New South Wales he held Drake responsible for the personal appearance of his officers, particularly Third Mate Baxter, as well as anyone responsible for serving rations to the prisoners. Finally, he ordered that the captain's logbook and/or journal of the voyage be forwarded to his office *that same day*. Lest the captain be in any doubt about Campbell's feelings, the colonial secretary also sent him a copy of his report to Macquarie on the state of the convicts following that routine muster.[129]

With the voyage ended, his ship moored in Port Jackson and the first procedural inspection complete, matters were now beyond the control of Captain John Drake. Campbell's letter of 2 August sealed his fate, at least in the short-to-medium term. The one thing that he had dreaded during that four-month voyage was losing control of his ship and all the people on board. Ironically, it took one short letter from a senior government bureaucrat in this far-flung colony to officially remove any and all remaining control over his vessel. Campbell's letters set in train a new set of events as Governor Macquarie and his judicial branch tried to figure out what exactly should be done in response to this ghastly voyage. Their challenge was immense.

Debating the options

One of the early obligations of the colonial government was to gather physical evidence in the case against various *Chapman* officers and soldiers. In the days following the disembarkation of the convicts and crew a small team of inspectors went on board to examine the prison. William Cosar, described as a master builder, Stephen Milton, Boatswain of the dockyard in Sydney and John Redman, the Chief Constable of Sydney, were deemed to be the best available experts for this task. Their brief was to survey the prison rather than the entire ship. Their report was clear and unambiguous. Following 'a careful and strict survey of the prison room and bulk heads belonging thereto', they found no evidence of an attempt to break open the doors from the inside. They detected no 'violence' towards the doors or the locks. They went on to declare that they believed the prison was in the same fortified condition as when it left England for Cork and New South Wales. The *Chapman* was 'fitted up' in the same way as most other vessels bringing convicts to the colony so they trusted their opinion that there had been no attempt at a breakout.[130] This analysis would fit with the fact that despite the many allegations during the journey that the convicts were attempting to break through their timber boundaries, there was no single report by the officers of damage to the locks or doors of the prison. Neither was there any report of the facility needing repair.

Captain Drake and his soon-to-be co-defendants quickly came to be regarded as criminals in danger of fleeing the colony. On 8 August, Secretary Campbell ordered John Piper, a government naval officer, to effectively lock down one of the key documents that would allow Drake to escape. Piper was commanded that under no account should he return the register of the ship to the possession of the captain or indeed to any other person outside of Campbell himself or Macquarie. 'The object of this injunction,' wrote Campbell, 'is to guard against any risk of the Master of the *Chapman* endeavouring to escape from the harbour, which would be facilitated by his possessing the register'.[131] From their first encounter it was clear that Campbell did not regard Drake either as a ship's commander or a person. His impetuous attitude toward the officials receiving the vessel under normal procedures in the colony made it difficult for him to explain the carnage of recent months.

As these processes of securing evidence and people continued during the following days, Macquarie and his officials consulted on a way forward. On 13 August, that path was laid down when the governor signed a warrant appointing a committee of inquiry to investigate the voyage. The document laid out some uncontested facts. The hired convict ship *Chapman* left Ireland under the command of Captain John Drake and was now moored in Sydney Cove. Several convicts met their death on the passage and many more received diverse wounds and injuries as a result of the use of firearms against them. Complaints were publicly made of cruelty, oppression and unjustifiable, improper and unauthorised treatment on the part of the officers in charge of the ship and convicts. It was now imperative upon the authorities to examine these charges quickly and in detail. The warrant appointed a Special Commission of Inquiry consisting of John Wylde L.L.B, who was the Judge Advocate of the colony. He was joined by John Thomas Campbell, Secretary to the Government, and D'Arcy Wentworth, a Justice of the Peace and Superintendent of the Police.[132]

Collectively these men represented a powerful force with considerable judicial clout. They were authorised to listen to, investigate and examine all relevant witness testimony, particulars and information that may be put before them in connection with the complaint. They were required to look at all of the incidents, circumstances and concerns connected in any way to the management of the vessel and the treatment of the prisoners. Their findings were to be published in a detailed report along with all the minutes of evidence. The warrant did not indicate whether the committee was required to make any recommendations regarding criminal charges but given that it requested 'findings' then this was likely the expectation.

On 15 August, Captain Drake received his formal notification to attend the committee of inquiry. The solicitor for the Crown, Thomas Wylde, detailed the need for the probe. The deaths of the convicts, the wounding of many others, the use of firearms by the soldiers, and the complaints of cruelty and oppression all warranted a detailed legal examination. The notification required Drake to attend the hearings, beginning the following Wednesday at 10 a.m. at the Governor's Court in the New Hospital Sydney.[133] Ironically, Thomas Wylde's son, John, would be one of those sitting in judgement of Drake and his people.

As was the normal course in such matters, several letters were exchanged between the three committee members as they were officially asked to submit their expertise to the inquiry. All three agreed to participate and the stage was set for a legal showdown. The build-up was not without some drama, however, as illustrated in a communication received by Campbell from Captain Drake. On Tuesday 19 August he wrote to inform the committee that several of his ship's company were being ill-treated in Sydney, particularly on the previous Sunday night when a number were 'unmercifully beaten and their lives threatened'.[134] He alleged that there was a great hostility directed toward himself and his crew and that they had heard whispers that they would be attacked on the way to court. With proceedings due to begin the following day, he implored Campbell to provide some form of police or military escort for him and his fellow officers and crew members as they travelled to and from the court building. On receipt of Drake's letter, Campbell wrote to his fellow committee member D'Arcy Wentworth in his role as Superintendent of Police to request two or more constables to receive the party from the ship the following morning and escort them to the Judge Advocate's Office.[135] He subsequently wrote to Drake and authorised him and his crew to land at the Governor's Wharf, where they would be given safe conduct to their destination and back again. This arrangement would continue for the duration of the inquiry.

Committee of Inquiry

Along with the aforementioned John Thomas Campbell, the committee set up to investigate the voyage was made up of two other considerable legal forces in the New South Wales colony. London-born John Wylde was appointed to the position of deputy judge-advocate of the territory and arrived there on 5 October 1816 on the ship *Elizabeth*. As a judge-advocate his role combined that of law officer, public prosecutor and judge. Among the legal reforms he introduced were a simplification of procedures, the creation of a supreme court in Van Diemen's Land, and the refusal to allow convict lawyers to practice in his court.[136] His role in the *Chapman* affair features in most accounts of his career but more significant than that was his part in the legal troubles of one of his fellow investigators, D'Arcy Wentworth.

One of the most colourful and influential figures in the early decades of British settlement in New South Wales, D'Arcy Wentworth was born near Portadown in Armagh around 1762. Prior to beginning a medical career, the young Wentworth served as an ensign in the First Armagh Company of the Irish Volunteers. Heavily influenced by the ideals of the American Revolution, he developed an immovable set of liberal ideals that shaped his thinking and decision-making when he later reached Australia. Alongside his work in the Volunteers he began serving a medical apprenticeship under Dr Alexander Patton from Tanderagee. With the possibility of a position with the East India Company, he travelled to London to continue his medical studies and while there he mingled with the crème de la crème of society. It is alleged that he fell into financial trouble due to a propensity for the good life and was charged three times at the Old Bailey sessions for highway robbery. He was found guilty on the first two occasions and acquitted for lack of evidence on the third. He appeared a fourth time, in December 1789, and was found not guilty yet again. The court was informed that he was in urgent need of release as he had secured a passage to Botany Bay.

From the time of his arrival at Port Jackson aboard the *Neptune* on 28 June 1790, Wentworth seemed destined to make his mark on the colony. He went on to hold posts as diverse as assistant at a hospital, superintendent of convicts, assistant surgeon in different grades, principal surgeon, justice of the peace, chief police magistrate, treasurer of the Police Fund, co-founder of the Bank of New South Wales and occasional 'inquisitor' in matters such as the tragedy of the *Chapman* voyage. Wentworth associated with several governors during his multi-faceted career, including a notable encounter with the despised William Bligh. It was his work with the progressive Lachlan Macquarie, however, that arguably marked the stand-out phase of his professional life. In another notable encounter, in 1817, Wentworth found himself in a legal wrangle with Lieutenant Colonel George Molle. Judge-Advocate John Wylde came to Wentworth's rescue by ruling that he, as surgeon, was not liable to court martial for the alleged offence.[137] The fact that later that same year, Wentworth and Wylde would sit together on a judicial panel to investigate the *Chapman* indicates the incestuous nature of high politics and bureaucracy in New South Wales during this period.

With the committee in place the inquiry began on 16 August. The exact structure of the public testimony is not known, though much of the evidence survives. All of the key players presented their version of the story to their three inquisitors. Led by Captain Drake, the 'defence' was supported by testimony from Surgeon-Superintendent Dewar, Chief Mate John Milbank, Officer of the Guard Busteed and Richard Drake, an officer and brother of the captain. Significantly absent from this hearing was one of the key protagonists, the notorious Third Mate Baxter.[138] In accordance with Campbell's initial recommendation, a number of convict witnesses presented their side of the story. Terence Kiernan spoke at considerable length, providing an extraordinary level of detail. Patrick Smith, the doctor's mate, gave his perspective. John Fagan, James Burn and John Ryan also spoke up on the convict side. Remarkably, the much-tortured William Leo survived to recount his gruesome tale, and he did so in great detail. Several ordinary sailors gave short accounts from their perspective and not surprisingly most incriminated the officers and soldiers. It appears that the convicts and sailors had a natural affinity during the voyage, most likely based on shared social status on land. This was one of the constant sources of suspicion for the officers and soldiers during the sailing.

On the first day of the inquiry Drake was instructed to put forward his own list of witnesses. From the officer class he proposed Lieutenant Busteed, First Mate John Milbank, Second Mate Robert Aldridge and Third Mate Baxter. Representing the sailors, he selected William Jones, John Weymouth, Alexander Johnston, Thomas Harris and Giffard Campion. Finally, from among the convicts he named Michael Collins, John Ryan, Michael Woods, James Cooper and James Brian, the latter two coming as prisoners on the *Pilot*.[139] Curiously, none of the ordinary crew members proposed as witnesses arose as players in any of the controversies recorded in the various diaries and journals compiled by Drake and Dewar.

Another drama played out alongside the public and private deliberations of the committee of inquiry. Once the suggestion of an inquiry was approved by Macquarie, an order was given that Captain Drake, the officers and crew should keep themselves available for the duration of any legal proceedings. As a result, the *Chapman* would remain moored in the harbour at Port Jackson and unable to proceed on an onward planned voyage to India. On 4 September, Drake wrote to Macquarie informing him that the ship was seaworthy again after the voyage from Ireland and had been readied for the next expedition. He reminded the governor that the ship was now sitting in the harbour at a cost of £400 per month. The continued detention would mean a loss of freight in India and a possible arrival 'at the breaking of the monsoon'. He was also concerned that the ship's owner would think the *Chapman* was being detained for his (Drake's) own private financial gain.[140]

This marked the beginning of a two-month war of words between Drake, Macquarie and Campbell as the *Chapman* remained an uncertain prisoner of the colonial government. On 8 September Campbell informed Drake that there was no detention order against him or the ship 'other than what arises from the circumstances now under investigation with the committee of enquiry'. Should nothing arise then the ship and those working on it were free to leave.[141] This proviso proved frustrating for Drake as it became clear that the ship was not being formally detained but rather being held hostage to an investigation that was taking far longer to complete than expected.

His polite fury with his would-be prosecutors reached something of a boiling point by mid-October. Writing again to Macquarie, he reminded the governor that the charges against himself and his officers had now been in place since 2 August. He gave notice on the last day of that month that the *Chapman* was ready for sea but two days later the ship was occupied by a detachment of soldiers, who announced that they had orders to fire on the officers and crew should they attempt to sail. He applied for the return of the ship's register on 24 September but this was referred to Macquarie for a decision. None was forthcoming. As far as Drake was concerned, the ship was under formal detention by the New South Wales government despite their official denial of that fact. He went on to repeat his concerns about the cost to his employers of the loss of business caused by the ship remaining inactive at Port Jackson and the potential commercial reputational damage to himself.[142]

Two weeks later, having received no reply, Drake again wrote to Macquarie and included his letter of 14 October. He emphasised the fact that the committee of inquiry was now close to three months into their investigation with no sign of conclusion.[143] As if to rub salt in Drake's wound, it was not Macquarie that finally responded but Campbell. He informed the captain that the governor had not been given his lengthy communication of two weeks earlier because he (Campbell) 'did not consider it necessary to trouble His Excellency with the peculiar circumstances of the case'.[144] He repeated the position that the *Chapman* was not in detention but the officers under investigation were not permitted to leave. In an almost provocative suggestion he made it clear that the ship could depart under normal regulations, should a suitable team be found to replace those connected with the inquiry.

Although cloaked in typically polite and bureaucratic language, there was no hiding Drake's consternation at the withholding of the 14 October letter from Macquarie. He responded to the governor that the ongoing denial that the *Chapman* was not in detention was 'an insult to the meanest understanding'. He lambasted the fact that the committee – appointed by the governor – had now been investigating a matter for three months when in fact this should have been concluded in a week. This was not a justification for a large ship being kept idle at enormous expense while occupied by a military guard. On 19 October he gave orders to the harbour master to unmoor the ship, but the corporal commanding the guard on board repeated the threat to prevent any movement.

Drake contended that it was unlikely that the presence of armed troops on the ship would not be possible without being so ordered by Macquarie. In a final dramatic attempt to move the process forward, he threatened that if there was not a satisfactory reply by the following Friday then he would surrender the *Chapman* entirely to the ownership of the colonial government, discharging the officers and crew.[145] With this threat Drake was clearly attempting to call the bluff of Macquarie, Campbell and their officials. Whether or not he was successful is not clear but it may be a coincidence that it was at this time that a problem emerged from the committee of inquiry. Ironically, the irate captain may have been justified in his annoyance over the delay.

Deadlock

In early November, Macquarie wrote to Judge-Advocate Wylde seeking an update on the progress of the committee's work. On 9 November, Wylde responded. He was working day and night and his committee work was only interrupted by the many other official demands on his time. Indeed, he described himself as 'much exhausted'. Given the friendship between Macquarie, Wylde, Wentworth and Campbell, it is not clear to what extent the next revelation would have been a bombshell to the governor. After hearing from multiple witnesses on all sides, spending weeks in deliberation and poring over logbooks and journals, the committee members could not reach agreement.[146] Interestingly, the division existed along the lines of those who visited the ship and saw the prison doors opened first-hand, and those who did not.

Whether or not emotion played any part in the thinking of John Thomas Campbell, the reality was that he was the one to board the vessel and saw the state of the inmates for himself. He also experienced the obstreperous behaviour of Captain Drake in those early hours of the first muster. His involvement with the *Chapman* was first-hand. Wylde and Wentworth decided, based on their second-hand evaluation of the situation, that the captain, the officer of the guard, the surgeon-superintendent, the chief mate and the second mate should not be held for trial in relation to the killing of the prisoners. Campbell did not agree with these findings. A report was not yet formally submitted to Macquarie as the three officials sought to find a common position. By 9 November, however, Wylde felt the situation was hopeless and that the best they could hope for was for he and Wentworth to submit one report and Campbell to submit another.[147] Six days later, Campbell, Wentworth and Wylde submitted their reports.

The Wentworth and Wylde judgements

Wentworth and Wylde seemed reluctant to apportion any blame to the captain and his officers without diluting it with the possibility that they may have *fairly* misinterpreted a difficult situation. The first key finding set the tone for the conclusion of their report. On the question of a prisoner conspiracy to kill the crew and take the ship, they found that there was no evidence to suggest that one ever existed. They inserted a proviso, however, that it was possible such a plan existed, but the evidence did not prove it. In a further effort to excuse the actions of the accused, they found that it was reasonable for the officers and soldiers to think there was a conspiracy from the moment that the convict Collins gave his evidence just after mid-April.[148] It was clear that Wentworth and Wylde knew that they could not apportion blame to the convicts for a conspiracy that did not exist. Yet they were unwilling to unconditionally blame the officers, who were, after all, fellow bureaucrats in service of the government.

The men could not ignore the evidence found by the port inspection team that the doors and walls of the ship were fully intact with no evidence of broken locks or timbers from the inside. They were forced to conclude, therefore, that there was no attempt by the convicts to break out of the prison. Despite the unequivocal nature of this fact, they continued to give the benefit of the doubt to the officers and soldiers. After all, it was reasonable to expect the reaction that ensued:

> when an attempt to break the prison actually takes place and the prison becomes then broken in our sight, then the evidence tends, in every little and single circumstance of the occasion, to satisfy as to the fact of a positive and absolute belief, entertained by every officer, soldier and sailor to a man that at that moment of the firing commencing and of the run or rush aft

by the prisoners on the 17th April, the prisoners were at that time putting into effect that intention of taking the ship, and, if taken, of murdering every one on board, which the crew and guard equally believed those prisoners deliberately and desperately on oath to have adopted.[149]

They claimed that the only cause of that first firing was the apprehension felt by the ship's personnel. This, they believed, was heightened by the fact that they were on a ship, at sea and at the mercy of such a large number of prisoners. They repeated that there was no attempted break-out but the gunfire was excusable on the grounds that heightened anxiety caused a misjudgement.[150] It appeared that this was not problematic for Wylde and Wentworth.

The finding on the shooting of 27–28 April was somewhat more critical of those working on the ship. Essentially the blame rested with an overzealous sentry who was unnerved when a number of prisoners refused to disperse from their conversation. 'The reasonableness therefore of this apprehension,' they declared, 'seems to be so much more questionable.'[151] In other words, if the sentries on duty outside the prison were not so trigger-happy and took a proper account of the situation before firing then this incident was preventable. Blame could only strongly be apportioned to those soldiers who fired the first shots and not so much to any who subsequently joined in. They could not have known that this was effectively a false alarm and so were only following the lead of their comrades. On this point the judges inexplicably came to the conclusion that despite the confusion and unprofessional behaviour, no criminal responsibility could be attached to any soldier for this incident. The officers were not responsible on the grounds that they all attempted to stop the firing as soon as it commenced. Their excusing of the soldiers was based on the fact that the firing stopped as soon as the false alarm was detected.

In their final summing up, the two judges commented on the treatment of the convicts during the voyage. It was true that they suffered greatly from punishments, violence, as well as loss of rest, comfort and liberty of every kind. They were denied their full rations for a large portion of the journey. In an almost farcical twist to such a comprehensive and detailed report they went on to declare that:

As it would be inconsistent and even absurd to consider these acts, whence these evils arose, as evidence of malice against the prisoners on the part of the crew and guard or any individuals on board, in respect of anything that happened on either occasion of the general firing.[152]

The officers, soldiers and crew were fully absolved of any criminality beyond a misdemeanour on the basis that up to 17 April the convicts had no complaints about their treatment. Punishments were few, rations were full and the voyage was largely peaceful. Anything that happened after the shooting was the result of suspicion and fear, and because of this the judges felt obliged to withhold any recommendation of prosecution.

'A cool, unbiased and impartial mind': The Campbell judgement

Campbell opened his dissenting report by apologising to Macquarie for the difficulty it caused. Although he and his two colleagues heard the same evidence and viewed the same written records, he took his own independent minutes of the witness testimony. When Judge-Advocate Wylde presented him with a copy of the official minutes as recorded by a legal clerk, Campbell claimed that there were 'some material variations between the evidence, recorded in that transcript, and in the minutes I had myself taken down with much care and attention.'[153] The government secretary was casting some doubt on the process and this was either an attempt to muddy the waters or a matter of genuine concern. He made his opinion on the case clear from the outset. There was no doubt in his mind 'of the high delinquency of the accused parties'. His initial declaration was sweeping. The shooting on convicts on three nights, 17 and 28 April and 24 May, as well as excessive corporal punishments, neglects, privations and cruelties 'exercised in a variety of forms toward unoffending men loaded with irons', along with close confinement, all added up to 'such systematic criminality, that I do most humbly conceive public justice cannot be satisfied unless the delinquents be brought or sent before a competent tribunal.'[154] He estimated that upwards of 4,000 lashes were administered during the voyage. While looking at the totality of punishments, neglects and cruelties he admitted that no single one of those events amounted to a capital offence. He insisted that 'a long-continued system of cruelty must stamp a determinate character on the more desperate acts, whereby so many fellow creatures were hurried out of life'. The only name for this, he believed, was 'wanton murder'.[155]

In a more forensic examination of the evidence Campbell went on to describe how he approached the matter with a 'cool, unbiased and impartial mind, devoid of prejudice'.[156] This statement may have been somewhat of a stretch, given that he was the only one of the three inquisitors to actually see the prisoners at first-hand when they stepped out of that dark prison at the end of July. He found that even if the notion of a possible convict mutiny was to be believed and accepted, the officers and soldiers did not take account of the reality that the men in the prison were very securely locked down in chains behind strongly secured doors. He astutely noted that given the location of the musket balls and the dead and injured prisoners, it was clear that none were in postures of offence near the prison doors but instead were all along the prison, some close to their berths.

He went on to criticise the officers for not effecting an appropriate response to the 'convict approvers' who provided surreptitious and false evidence of a convict plot. Even if this evidence had been credible, there were steps that could have been taken to meet an attack from the prison. No extra watches were appointed. No additional military guards were placed around the prison. This was particularly significant in light of the first shooting, when Collins had come forward a day or two beforehand. Campbell claimed that their lack of preparedness indicated that the officers placed no trust in his evidence. He was not believed by them at the time yet they used him afterwards as a justification for their behaviour and that of the soldiers.

Campbell's unforgiving report tackled one particular individual that was neglected in the final summation of his two colleagues. The influence of Third Mate James Baxter was felt all over the ship during the voyage, particularly among the soldiers and ordinary crew members. He was responsible for gathering the crucial intelligence from convicts Collins and Ryan and he passed this on to Captain Drake. Baxter, Campbell contended, 'was all along most particularly forward and active in his work of destruction.'[157] For Campbell this did not absolve Drake from his duty in maintaining authority over the ship he was commanding and his drunkenness was not an excuse for his criminal neglect, but rather an aggravating factor. Neither were the surgeon-superintendent or senior military officer any less responsible for the 'apathy and indifference' they demonstrated when they stood by in a 'cold blooded manner' and witnessed the death and punishments 'in so wanton and barbarous a manner', particularly of William Leo. They were equally guilty and implicated. On top of this, he added their complicity in the withholding of rations as another indicator of their 'delinquency' in the whole affair.

In his final analysis, Campbell named those he pronounced to have the greatest levels of responsibility for the massacre and tortures on the *Chapman*. Captain Drake, Surgeon-Superintendent Dewar and Lieutenant Busteed were chiefly responsible because they held the highest responsibilities on the ship. They should be sent to England as prisoners and put on trial. First Mate Milbank, Second Mate Aldridge and Third Mate Baxter were 'actively engaged in the atrocities' and should also be sent to England and put on trial. Soldiers Clements, Hogan and Jordan also held responsibility and should be sent back; he noted that all three were in confinement in Sydney at this time. For an English court to ascertain the facts it would also be necessary for a number of witnesses to be sent home. He recommended that Terence Kiernan, Patrick Smith, Michael Woods and John Fagan should be returned along with the sailors Cornelius Crawley and William Nelson.[158] The problem with Campbell's decisive recommendation was that it threw a legal spanner in the works. With Wylde and Wentworth having adopted a wholly divergent opinion, three of the most powerful figures in the colony of New South Wales were deadlocked over the fate of the most senior officers of the *Chapman*.

6

Judgement

The *Chapman* was a veritable floating hell. Governor Macquarie's official inquiry revealed horrors that rival any in the darkest pages of Australia's earliest history. The decks were stained with the blood of twelve convicts killed during the nightmare voyage. Her suffocating sick-bay was crowded with twenty other half-naked wretches suffering from gunshot and bayonet wounds.[159]

This summary of the nightmare of the *Chapman* was published in a Brisbane newspaper 137 years after the event. If this broad outline was to be accepted, then the question arises as to why two-thirds of the committee found it difficult to identify even one person eligible for prosecution. By commissioning an inquiry to investigate the March–July 1817 voyage of the *Chapman* from Cork to New South Wales, Governor Lachlan Macquarie hoped for a timely and definitive resolution to the affair. When that inquiry ended in legal stalemate the poison chalice that he had handed to his friends just months earlier was promptly handed back to the reforming bureaucrat. In hindsight there was probably never a question as to what path Macquarie would take once the logjam had arisen. As a governor he believed in his duty to enable not only the punishment but also the reformation of the convicts. He was particularly well-disposed toward the idea of rewarding convicts for good behaviour, whether with land grants or judicial appointment.[160] This did not endear him to his government paymasters back in London. In 1814 he initiated a process to end the practice of convicts who were employed in the various urban areas of Sydney and beyond being allowed to stay in private lodgings at night. Despite the rejections of the British government, a barracks was opened in June 1819 for the purpose of boarding convicts under supervision at night-time.[161] While he did have a penchant for flogging and execution, he was a governor who often demonstrated compassion and humanitarianism. His next move in the *Chapman* affair did nothing to ingratiate himself to the London government.

Two days after receiving both sets of reports from the inquiry, he wrote a formal response to Judge-Advocate Wylde. His position was as uncompromising as his dissent. He could not in any way agree with the findings of Wylde or Wentworth. They found, in his interpretation, that there was no ground for instigating criminal proceedings against any of the parties subjected to the investigation. He disagreed vehemently:

> For after all that has taken place and appears so fully in evidence, I cannot possibly entertain a doubt as to the criminality of the proceedings on board the *Chapman*, which appears to me as marked with unparalleled cruelty and atrocity, wantonly inflicted and totally unprovoked on the part of the convicts, in some degree originating in and ascribable to the unfounded and pusillanimous apprehensions of the parties concerned.[162]

In what would by modern standards be an extraordinary legal intervention, Macquarie urged Wylde to reassemble his committee and reach a different conclusion. He requested that the supreme court judge Barron Field be asked to join the committee and offer his legal opinion. Judge Field, a direct descendant of Oliver Cromwell, came to New South Wales in 1816 on the female convict ship *Lord Melville*.[163] Macquarie was initially enamoured of Field, who shared the governor's reforming spirit. In encouraging his participation in the *Chapman* reporting process, it is possible he was hoping for a like-minded opinion.

Macquarie was particularly concerned with the fate of Captain Drake, Surgeon-Superintendent Dewar, the military officers and the three mates. He singled out Baxter as having been 'the most active and sanguinary in the long series of cruelties and atrocities committed on board the *Chapman*'.[164] The governor essentially ordered Wylde to consult with Wentworth and Field, revisit the entire report, and bring it into line with the opinions of Campbell and himself. He should also do this with haste.

Even in a far-flung early nineteenth-century colonial township with an infant legal system, Macquarie's next intervention could best be described as unethical. That same day he wrote to Judge Field setting out his thoughts on the inquiry reports. He described his 'utter astonishment' that Wylde and Wentworth had found no grounds for criminal charges against the officers of the ship and offered no proposal to send them back to England for a trial. In repeating his exasperation at 'a lawyer of Mr Judge Advocate Wylde's professional knowledge and experience' he indicated that he had read the report and all the accompanying documents. He could only conclude that several individuals on board the ship were criminally liable for their actions. The logbooks and journals of the captain and surgeon seemed to be particularly incriminating, in his opinion. After revealing his own observations on the reports with some considerable force of his words, Macquarie concluded by asking Judge Field to offer his own 'able legal assistance'.[165] The implication was unmistakable; he wanted Field to intervene as an independent legal professional but in reality to act on the governor's behalf and boost the findings of Campbell.

Judge Field, however, had already acquainted the committee with his feelings on three separate occasions during their investigation. After reading the first two volumes of evidence he was quite clear in his legal opinion. He recommended that Captain Drake, Surgeon-Superintendent Dewar, along with Aldridge, Baxter, Clements, Blucher, Wardrop, Mayne Hooper and Jordan – the latter four being privates of the 46th Regiment – should all be sent back to London and be indicted for murder at the High Court of Admiralty. Field believed that the case against the aforementioned was strengthened based on the evidence of those who did not allege ill-treatment during the voyage. Even at this early stage of the inquiry he observed that the committee members were placing far too much emphasis on the false impression held by the officers, soldiers and crew that the prisoners were about to try and seize the ship. He noted that because there was no overt act of breaking out of the prison the sailors and soldiers could not proceed 'at any time they pleased, in wantonly taking away the lives of the convicts merely because they were bona-fide persuaded the convicts had intended to take away theirs.'[166] If the principle of acting because something *might* happen was deemed acceptable, then what was to stop the soldiers and sailors from suffocating all the convicts at once? He described this as 'the doctrine of excuse by reason of sincere persuasion of intention to murder'. He concluded this stage of his analysis by declaring that until the broader crew of the *Chapman* could prove a rush of prisoners towards the door or an attempted break-out on each occasion on which there was shooting, then those doing the shooting should be indicted as murderers. Even a belief that they were about to be murdered, he argued, did not give an equal right to the shooters to carry out the same act. Belief was not sufficient for a defence.

In his second update eleven days later, the judge was unwavering. In referencing the convict testimony he had previously reviewed, he returned to the idea of a possible mutiny from within the prison:

> The question is not whether the free men believed the convicts intended to take the ship, which I make no doubt the former did believe, and think it very likely the latter did intend, as perhaps there never was a ship fully of convicts yet that did not intend, if they could.[167]

Field found the testimony now available from soldiers and sailors to be more interesting. From their words he remained unconvinced of a prison break-out and it was clear that no prisoner had come close to making his way up on deck. While he agreed that the second shooting was an acknowledged mistake, he had a common problem with both events. Even if the soldiers were distressed by the darkness of the hatchways into which they were firing, there was no justification for continuing beyond the initial shots. In the 17 April event the shots continued for around half an hour. In the second shooting it was fifteen minutes. How could this be justified when the absence of danger was established so quickly, he asked. He attributed the killing of Lucy during the 24 May incident as a murder committed by Private Hogan.

By the end of the first week of October, Field had finished reading all the evidence. He had developed the opinion that there was definitely a plot by the prisoners to take the ship. Furthermore, the crew and soldiers earnestly believed that such a mutiny plot existed. The initial moments of the first firing could, therefore, be legally classified as a misadventure. Citing a number of unrelated legal cases, he reverted to an earlier proviso that the problem with both the first and second shootings was not their inception but their duration. 'Long after any reasonable apprehension of danger, such killing would be murder,' he wrote. According to Dewar's journal, the first firing continued for up to an hour, while witness testimony claimed about thirty minutes. Either way it was well beyond the threshold for identifying a false alarm and this was what turned these apparently defensive measures into criminal events.

Field decreed that the committee should give Macquarie the opportunity to send all those who fired shots on 17 April, as well as their 'abettors', back to England where they should face a jury. He saw only scant evidence that would allow the captain and the surgeon to face such serious charges. He believed, however, that both men held positions of ultimate responsibility over the care of the convicts and it was necessary that they too should be sent home, either as witnesses or defendants. Drawing attention to discrepancies in Dewar's accounts of various happenings on the ship, Field pointed out that the language in his daily journal was framed quite differently to his subsequent testimony. In the diary his phrases were short and failed to illustrate the wider picture. In his testimony he spoke about his and Drake's efforts to stop the shooting and the cries of mercy from the convicts. Lieutenant Busteed should also be sent home because of his failure to control his men.

Judge Field declined Macquarie's request to join the committee or indeed to hold meetings with its members after they became deadlocked. He informed the governor that he had already provided his opinion to the three members privately during those three occasions and would be willing to make them public if required.[168] Judge-Advocate Wylde, meanwhile, appeared to become exasperated with Macquarie's attitude, particularly as the case had already added considerably to his already excessive workload. In response to his letter of 17 November, later that same evening he reminded the governor that he had spent the day at a court martial and was already fatigued from his 'unceasing public duties'.[169] Despite this, he felt obliged to correct Macquarie's interpretation of one aspect of the report. Under no circumstances did the report intend to indicate that there should be no criminal charges arising from the events on the voyage. Rather, he suggested, the report indicated that there was not enough evidence to bring charges of murder against the captain, the surgeon-superintendent or the officer of the guard.

Wylde hit back somewhat forcibly at Macquarie, arguing that he was at a loss as to what he was expected to do with a report that was the product of weeks of 'arduous and painful attention'. He agreed to reassemble the committee immediately and listen once more to the views of John Thomas Campbell in the hope that he may convey the governor's specific concerns. He promised to at least try and bring his own views more into line with the Macquarie–Campbell positions.[170] In making one further attempt to bring about a satisfactory conclusion – from his viewpoint – to the *Chapman* affair, Macquarie was guided by two factors. In bureaucratic terms the matter had been on his desk since the end of July and was consuming far too much time. To compound the urgency, the convict vessel *Harriet* was scheduled to leave Sydney for England on 30 November; he wanted any prisoners and their paperwork on that ship and out of his sight.

The decision

With the clock ticking, the committee reconvened to deliberate the report in an attempt to identify any common ground between the opposing viewpoints. The deliberation was short; clearly an exercise designed to assure Macquarie that the three parties had at least gone through the motions. Wentworth and Wylde did not change their positions. Not only did they believe in the accuracy of their position but they saw no cause to revise any element of the conclusions. As the last week of November began, Wylde and Macquarie became embroiled in a tense, albeit polite, round of communications as they worked through the various legal complexities of the *Chapman* case. The debate became protracted, focussing on the types of charges that may be brought, the specific motivations behind the three significant shooting events, and the dispersal of punishments among the convicts. In frustration and possibly arising from exhaustion, something he referred to more than once, Wylde reminded the governor that it was he who had helped him draft the warrant that set up the inquiry in the first place. He noted that it was his intention that the committee should only establish facts and not necessarily furnish recommendations on further action. This, he stated, was purely in the hands of the governor. Those facts, as found by the majority of the three-person committee, included the finding that there was no crime committed during the voyage of the *Chapman*. Whether this was merely a formula of words designed by Wylde to give Macquarie a path to criminal charges is almost impossible to confirm.

With the stand-off nearing a conclusion, it only remained for the parties to find an agreeable legal path to resolution. On 24 November, Wylde further conceded that Macquarie held full and final authority regarding the fate of the soon-to-be-accused. He concurred that Lieutenant Busteed, Surgeon Dewar, Captain Drake and the three mates, John Milbank, Robert Aldridge and James Baxter, should all be returned to England to face criminal charges.[171] The soldiers, Jordan, Hogan and Clements, were already confirmed for return, where they would be charged with murder. This gave rise to a new round of polite squabbling between the officials, however, as they debated the means by which the various accused individuals should be transported. The options appear to have been 'close military arrest' or as conventional prisoners. Again there was disagreement, but by the end of the month Macquarie conceded that Dewar and Busteed could travel under military arrest. He insisted that Third Mate Baxter, owing to the nature of his behaviour on the ship, should be sent home as a prisoner.

The final significant action to be taken in this now three-month investigative process was the selection of witnesses for the prosecution. Macquarie and his senior law officers knew it would be pointless sending home the prisoners with bundles of written evidence alone. First-hand testimony would be required in order to support the prosecutions that would eventually be brought. Wylde suggested, and Macquarie accepted, the following list of witnesses:

Sailors
Giffard Campion, Cornelius Crawley, Henry Jennings, Peter Cocker, William Nelson, Robert Kirby, William Jones, John Fierdaunt, John Clift, Michael Arnold, Alexander Johnson.

Soldiers
Alexander Wardrope, George Cooke, Robert Vickery, John Brown,
William Hutchins, John Hooper, Thomas Turner, Edward Jo, Michael
Desmond, William Hawkins, John Young.

Convicts
Patrick Smith, Peter Allan, John Sullivan, John Fagan, Michael Wood,
Terence Kiernan, John Ryan, Francis Murphy, Thomas Kelly, James
Talbot, Michael Collins, William Leo.

From 1 December, with all key decisions finally made, the task of
informing those being returned got under way. Busteed and Dewar were
notified, by identical letters, that they were to be returned to England
under close military arrest. They were further ordered to consider themselves under open arrest and remain ready to board the ship *Harriet* at
short notice.[172] Busteed acknowledged the letter and submitted to the
fact that he was under arrest and promised to remain in readiness.[173]
Dewar responded in a similar manner, but with a possible combination of
pomposity and self-indulgence whereby he effectively demanded that he
be provided with quarters equal to those befitting the rank he held in the
Navy.[174] It is not clear whether his requirements were met but the surgeon persisted in challenging his prosecutors in whatever way possible. In
wanting to adhere to the *Instructions from the Transport Board*, he demanded
that his medical journal and diary be returned to him before departing
New South Wales. Those instructions required that he surrender these
documents in the normal way, having returned from a convict transportation voyage. Either the erstwhile surgeon did not understand that he
was not returning home in the conventional fashion, or he was trying to
inconvenience the colonial officials with endless streams of correspondence. Either way, he was informed that he would not be receiving his
records because they would be required for evidence in any forthcoming
prosecutions in England.

A new destination

On 21 December 1817, more than a year after leaving the naval dockyard at Deptford, the *Chapman* finally set sail from New South Wales, many months behind schedule. In a somewhat extraordinary twist, Captain Drake and his three mates were once again in command of the vessel as it set a course for its intended destination in the Dutch East Indies. They were accompanied by a number of petty officers and sailors from the voyage from Cork, but Drake and his three mates were effectively travelling on a form of bail whereby they were expected to surrender to the authorities in London once the *Chapman* finished its business. The following day, after almost five months of legal oblivion, an eclectic troupe of former *Chapman* crew and prisoners departed New South Wales on the *Harriet*. Under the command of Captain Jones, the ship carried a cargo of New Zealand pine, fur seal skins, and 'wool of colonial growth'. Some fifteen members of the passenger list were part of the *Chapman* convict party, now travelling as prosecution witnesses.[176] Along with these individuals were James Clements, John Hogan and John Jordan, all of whom were charged with murder. The former surgeon-superintendent of the *Chapman*, Alexander Dewar, and the former commander of the military guard, Lieutenant Busteed, were also on board, travelling under close military arrest. Ten soldiers also travelled on the *Harriet* as witnesses.[177]

With the *Chapman* headed for Batavia – modern-day Jakarta – and the *Harriet* taking the now well-travelled route back to England, the entire episode was finally removed from the shoulders of Macquarie, Campbell, Wentworth and Wylde. All that is known of the journey back to England is that the ship made a stop-over at the Cape of Good Hope. The journey will have been particularly isolating and possibly humiliating for the former surgeon Dewar, who was now increasingly isolated, having been separated from two of his key protectors, Captain Drake and Third Mate Baxter. In a letter to the English authorities outlining the reasons for returning this human cargo to London, Macquarie declared:

> Altho' I cannot but despair of effectual Justice being rendered by the mode
> I have, under the Advice of the Judge Advocate, been induced to adopt, yet
> I still hope that sufficient may be effected at least to protect the persons
> of Convicts and violence, to which they have been heretofore in a certain

degree exposed, chiefly owing to the rude and boisterous description of Men who generally command Merchant Ships, And to the little care they take to prevent their petty Officers from exercising tyrannical and unnecessary Severities towards them.[178]

There was never any doubt about Governor Macquarie's motives and persistence in the face of the traditional attitude of officialdom towards convicts. This declaration was in keeping with his broader actions and sentiments during the entirety of his governorship. How favourably his declaration would be received in London would have definitive consequences for Drake, Dewar, Busteed and the other defendants.

January 1819: Three days at the Old Bailey

The saga of the *Chapman* touched off a third calendar year when the purpose of the reverse transportation of several officers and soldiers from the Cork to New South Wales voyage of almost two years earlier finally reached its legal culmination. A drama that began quietly in the Cove of Cork before moving across oceans and hemispheres, to the colony of New South Wales, had now shifted back to the seat of the empire where it would ultimately be resolved. Between 1536 and 1834, naval offences committed on English ships were usually tried at special sessions of the Court of Admiralty in London. This medium 'ensured that the seas were not entirely lawless'.[179] Among the key responsibilities that this forum dealt with were criminal and civil matters related to the sea. The necessity to defeat piracy was one of the original reasons for its establishment during the medieval period. It typically heard cases involving murder, sodomy, theft, slaving and swindles involving vessels that were deliberately sunk after being heavily insured, as well as some lesser matters.[180] When Macquarie and Campbell wrote of a 'competent court' in which to try those accused in the *Chapman* case, this was the only legally realistic option.

On 11 January 1819 the first of the defendants were put to the bar before the magistrates and jury at the Admiralty Sessions, held at the Old Bailey. James Clements, one of the soldiers, and the former captain John Drake were charged with the wilful murder of John McArdle on 28 April off St Jago.[181] Somehow, the charge against Drake was promoted to murder between the time of his leaving New South Wales and stepping into this courtroom. Just after two o'clock in the afternoon, Sir Christopher Robinson rose to speak. Robinson was a long-time specialist in maritime law and King's Advocate and one of the leading counsel at the Admiralty Court.[182] He argued that there was no more troubling a case to come before a court than the one against John Drake and James Clements. The question, he believed, was whether the men had exceeded the power entrusted to them in their functions on the *Chapman*. Outlining the bare known facts of the voyage, the departure from Cork, the dates of the alleged offences and the subsequent loss of life, he revealed that Drake had submitted himself to arrest that very day.[183] After outlining the evidence in the case of Drake and Clements, he called his first witness. Terence Kiernan, who provided some of the most detailed eyewitness testimony to Campbell, Wentworth and Wylde back in New South Wales, was now front and centre amidst all the intimidating splendour of the learned gentlemen of the Admiralty Sessions. The Common Serjeant, representing the prisoners, rose to argue that the court should be provided with the details of the convictions that placed the former convict witnesses on the *Chapman* in the first place. This was clearly an attempt to discredit those witnesses in the eyes of the magistrates. When they heard that Terence Kiernan was once convicted of grand larceny at a court in Drogheda, would it further diminish their trust in his testimony? Just another Irish scoundrel. This process was repeated each time a former *Chapman* convict gave evidence at the Admiralty Sessions.

Terence Kiernan was questioned at length about his experiences on the voyage. From the moment he and roughly twenty other convicts were transported to the *Chapman* on board a small boat in Cork, to his front-and-centre account of the shootings on 17 and 28 April, his story did not diverge from the one told to colonial government officials in the autumn of 1817. Kiernan appeared to fare well under cross-examination, repeatedly denying that he possessed or used knives or cutting implements. While outlining his version of the events of the day and evening of 17 April, he reminded the court that he could not be certain of the day because he was not allowed to possess any writing material. The threat was very clear; any convict detected with writing in his possession would be taken up on deck and executed.[184] He recounted an episode where he earned himself a double flogging for speaking to Dr Dewar in Latin. He did concede that he had no idea whether Clements fired the shot that killed McArdle because he could not see him; his theory was based on the fact that he could only hear his voice in the vicinity from which the shot emerged. Perhaps the most stunning news to emerge from Kiernan's testimony was the fact that the notorious Third Mate James Miles Baxter would not be facing trial because he died on the passage from Australia back to London.[185] In the most ironic twist of fate, it is likely that Baxter was buried at sea.

Testifying on the shooting event at the end of April, Kiernan described the moment when Baxter and some of the soldiers later walked among the convicts. Presumably with the light provided by their torches, he discovered that his mess-mate, John McArdle, lay fatally wounded in his berth. A bullet (or ball) had entered his lower stomach and was lodged in his body. He estimated that the shot that killed McArdle came from the direction of the soldiers' apartment. Speaking of his broader experience on the voyage, Kiernan claimed that the soldiers had frequently 'ill-used' the convicts, to such an extent that he himself avoided going up on deck to receive his allocation of wine.[186]

The next witness in the case against Drake and Clements was Thomas Kelly. His testimony tallied with that of Kiernan. His berth was close to that of Kiernan and the late John McArdle. Kelly himself was badly wounded in the shooting while his brother was killed in the same incident in which McArdle died.[187] Under cross-examination he confirmed that his irons were not broken on 17 April, but one of them 'was off'. For this, he was flogged on deck and witnessed twenty other convicts punished in the same way and for the same offence. He denied seeing a concealed Bible anywhere on board to facilitate the taking of oaths. Convict Michael Woods was the next witness and he revealed his perspective on the different events from his berth near the main hatchway. He confirmed that the sole voice he could hear directly outside or near the main hatchway was that of Clements, making various threats about noise from the convicts. When the convict irons were inspected on 17 April his were intact and so he escaped punishment. He estimated, however, that about thirty-four or thirty-five inmates had their irons removed at the direction of Dr Dewar. Yet it was Dr Dewar, he claimed, who ordered that those inmates be flogged for having their irons removed.[188]

After hearing from the convicts, it was time for the court to receive testimony from some of the soldiers. John Brown testified that he was on duty on 28 April when he heard 'a great rushing down below'. In the melee he was told that the convicts had got up on deck but when the firing began he did not know who was pulling the triggers. Under cross-examination he revealed that the soldiers slept 'on their arms' – presumably meaning with their weapons close at hand – for a full six weeks as they feared being murdered by the convicts. He confirmed the fears that existed from among his ranks with regard to the ordinary sailors. Noting that Lucy and Nelson were kept in irons for most of the voyage, he claimed that picklock keys were found on Crawley, who was also held in detention.

Private George Cooke claimed that the ship would have been taken and the soldiers and crew murdered on 28 April had the soldiers not fired in defence. He claimed to have heard the convicts declare 'fire away, and be damned to you, till your ammunition be gone, and we will get the ship'.[189] He went on to incorrectly testify that the convicts broke down a door in their charge towards the bulkhead, leaving very little by means of a barrier between them and the magazine where the arms and ammunition were stored. Had this succeeded then they would have taken control of the weapons and the ship, allowing them to carry out the conspiracy outlined by Michael Collins. He contended that the vessel was to be attacked when seventeen convicts were on deck but the plan was thwarted by the fact that William Leo, one of the ringleaders, was handcuffed at the opportune moment.

On this charge against Clements and Drake, the prosecution ended. One of the judges, Mr Justice Park, decided that there was no evidence against Captain Drake and, therefore, he should not be called to testify. Likewise, he saw no reason to call Clements. After some undefined but short period of consultation he and his fellow magistrates, Sir William Scott and Mr Justice Best, announced that they had reached similar conclusions. The evidence given by the three convicts could not have been more contradictory and indeed, such 'incredible declarations had never been heard in a Court of Justice'.[190] The court found that there was a conspiracy on board the *Chapman* and that Drake and Clements were justified in firing to defend themselves. The jury found both men not guilty.

This was not, however, the end of the case. There were further charges to be examined by the judges and jury. Before finishing this first day of events, the grand jury presented a true bill found against Drake, Dewar and Lieutenant Christopher Busteed for murder. Dewar had already surrendered himself and both he and Drake were remanded to Newgate Prison until the following morning. The court refused bail. The now-exonerated soldier James Clements was fully discharged while the three convict witnesses were ordered to be kept in custody until the following day.

The next morning, John Drake was back before the Admiralty Sessions judges and jury, again facing a charge of murder. His co-defendants were Dr Dewar and Lieutenant Busteed. They were accused of the murder of Daniel McCormack on board the *Chapman* sometime during April 1817. Once again Sir Christopher Robinson laid out the case and it mirrored much of what had been stated the previous day. Patrick Smith, a convict and the doctor's mate, was the first witness. He described the presence of bullet holes in the timberwork separating the sickbay from the soldiers' apartments as a result of the 17 April shooting. Curiously, he claimed that after the main shooting ended, the third mate 'came down and fired among the convicts'.[191] If with this statement he was claiming that Baxter physically entered the prison and fired at the convicts point blank, then this is the first mention of that allegation. He also alleged that the second mate, Aldridge, fired into the sickbay. Again this appears to be the first time that this piece of news reached any official enquiry.

Under intense cross-examination, Smith revealed some hitherto obscure details of the voyage. He insisted that he heard no rush of convicts towards the prison door during the shooting episodes and that, from his location in the sickbay, he would surely have heard such disturbances. He reiterated his claim that one portion of the timberwork adjoining the sickbay door was marked with as many as fourteen bullet holes. This was in support of his argument that Second Mate Aldridge did fire at the room. Smith recalled that Michael Collins came under a real threat from his fellow convicts as a result of his conversations with Surgeon Dewar. Although not carried out, there was an indication that the informer was to be 'blanketed' by those he betrayed. Blanketing involved placing a blanket over the head of the victim and smothering them. Smith revealed another incident where an unnamed convict suffered a number of broken ribs as a result of a physical argument with a younger man.

The proceedings heard from several further convict witnesses, all attempting to convince the court of the innocence of the body of convicts in the face of oppression and victimisation. John Fagan gave evidence of the colourful language of Captain Drake and the nonchalant attitude of Surgeon Dewar toward the sick and wounded. Like almost every other convict witness, he claimed to know nothing of oath-taking or broken chains. Francis Murphy confirmed other convict accounts of the day and evening of 17 April; they were mustered for the distribution of wine in the morning and all was normal until they settled down for the night. Like Fagan, he claimed that Drake, as well as Dewar and Busteed, all bated the convicts with threats and provocative language from the other side of the timber walls and doors of their prison. Under cross-examination Murphy denied the claim made by Michael Collins at sea that he (Murphy) was to become the surgeon after the murder of Dewar. Upon re-examination he claimed that Drake and Dewar both promised to flog him at every opportunity and hang him at the yard-arm when they reached Sydney.[192] Peter Allan, described as 'a man of colour', heard Corporal Cooke inform Captain Drake on the evening of 17 April that there were men at the hatchway; immediate orders were given to fire.[193] The following morning he was confronted by Drake, who directed him to prepare for death. A pistol was held to his chest and he was asked to name the ringleaders of the planned mutiny.

John Ryan was the one convict, along with Collins, who claimed to have knowledge of a convict takeover of the ship. Under cross-examination he recounted how he told Dewar and Drake of the existence of five would-be ringleaders who planned their attack for 17 April. Under this plan, Dewar would be the first to be murdered, with Murphy taking over. Now, in a courtroom in London in January 1819, he retracted the entire story. Explaining the discrepancies in his accounts, he claimed that he told this story on the ship and again in New South Wales because he feared for his life. Following the 17 April shooting he claimed that Dewar took him into a small room with Collins and told him a lengthy tale. Dewar promised him money to recount this story as sworn evidence while Drake assured him that it would save his life.

The final convict witness to any legal proceeding associated with the voyage of the *Chapman* was William Leo. Describing his now infamous and prolonged torture, he explained how he was taken up on deck subsequent to the first firing event. After being placed on his knees and instructed that he was being given ten final minutes of life during which he should pray, he was charged with being a ringleader in the alleged conspiracy. Following a severe flogging, Dr Dewar ordered that a rope be placed around his body, whereupon he was dropped into the sea and towed behind the ship. When he was eventually retrieved from the water, in a perilous state, he was brought to the poop deck, where he remained for fifteen days, fully exposed to the elements. At the end of that period he was flogged again. Under cross-examination he confirmed that he eventually told Dewar that Francis Murphy intended to take the ship but only to end his torture and save his own life. He testified that he told Drake that he himself was to be the armourer but was unsure who would take over the other functions.[194] With this testimony William Leo claimed that he essentially told the senior officers what they wanted to hear, but only did so after experiencing extreme torture. The various accounts of his torture were among the most consistent in all the witness testimonies throughout the different legal proceedings investigating the voyage.

Next it was the turn of the soldier witnesses. Thomas Turner was on guard with eleven others on the evening of 17 April. They already had orders to fire if they noticed convicts trying to break out from the prison. At one point he heard a 'rush' of one group of prisoners going forward and another going in the opposite direction, as if they were attempting to storm the perimeter of their penitentiary. He called out to enquire what the noise was but received no response; some of the other soldiers shouted to him and each other that the convicts were breaking the bulkhead. It was then that the shooting began, but he heard no orders given. He claimed the firing lasted just fifteen minutes, after which time the convicts were heard begging for mercy. He testified that he did not see any of the prisoners during the firing. Under cross-examination he seemed to contradict this by claiming that he saw up to twenty of them walking around fully dressed. He contended that the rattling of the chains, during the initial 'rush' that he and others could not see, proved that such a movement was indeed under way beneath their feet. During many musters, he claimed, much damage was detected in the irons restraining the convicts, and he described how rivets were out of place, rings of the irons were twisted off, and many were immediately broken after being repaired. 'The conduct of the prisoners,' he concluded, 'was very outrageous.'[195] Turner claimed to be in constant fear that the ship would be taken by the convicts. He estimated that it would take twenty men to force the bulkhead and reach the armoury, at which point they would have full control over the ship.

For a further military perspective on that first shooting, the court heard from one final witness. Richard Vickery was a soldier on duty on the evening in question. He heard 'a great noise' and the breaking open of a door. It was burst off its hinges and he could hear a 'violent rushing' take place.[196] Every soldier was called to arms and they received orders to fire. In an indication of how rattled the crew and soldiers might have been, he described how, on one night alone, they were raised from their sleep four times to answer different potential alarms. The problem with Vickery's testimony – and this was not raised in court – is that there was no account of a broken door having been separated from its hinges. If the accounts of those who inspected the ship after it arrived in Sydney were to be accepted, then this part of Vickery's testimony was unsound.

Case closed

With the conclusion of this line of testimony the main prosecutor, King's Advocate Sir Christopher Robinson, told the court that he had other evidence but none that could carry the case forward. This suggests that the remaining evidence may have been repetitive or it could also indicate a lack of interest in successfully prosecuting the case. Twenty-four months after the *Chapman* arrived in Cork, twenty-two months after it departed from Cork, twenty months after the first prisoner died at the hands of the soldiers of the 46th Regiment, the case concluded. Under the direction of the honourable Mr Justice Best of the Admiralty Session, the jury acquitted John Drake, Alexander Dewar and Christopher Busteed of any remaining charges related to the blood-soaked voyage of the *Chapman*. Three soldiers brought to the court by *habeas corpus* were also ordered to be discharged. These directions brought the entire legal saga of the voyage and its attendant horrors to a conclusion.

7

After the *Chapman*

With the multiple judicial inquiries into the voyage of the *Chapman* concluded in favour of the officers, soldiers and crew, the question remains as to the legacy of the voyage. By the time Drake and Dewar walked free from the Old Bailey, those convicts who survived the journey and disembarked at the end of July 1817 had long since been absorbed into colonial life. How did any convict transition from a life of impoverishment in Ireland, by means of a turbulent voyage across hemispheres and into a new existence in a world that was almost as alien as anything in the known universe? For the two most powerful figures on the ship, Captain Drake and Surgeon-Superintendent Dewar, the verdicts at the Admiralty Sessions brought closure to what was likely the most turbulent period in either man's naval careers. Their challenge was to re-establish their reputations in a post-*Chapman* life, hoping that the scandal of being charged with murder and various associated offences would not prove damaging to their future prospects.

This chapter will explore the futures that unfolded for some of those involved in what turned out to be one of the most shameful episodes in the physical removal of convicts from Ireland to New South Wales. It is not possible to trace the fate of every convict or crew member. Only sketchy evidence survives of the number who were granted pardons or land. Likewise, determining the after-histories of those high-profile member of the crew also proves difficult with the passage of time. The

Nelsons and Crawleys of the voyage were never rated much higher than the convicts they were employed to transport and so they tended to disappear into the deep well of historical anonymity that was so often reserved for the poor and unknown. The chapter will open with an appraisal of the systems of disposing of convicts who arrived successfully in New South Wales, along with some limited data on the fate of the men who populated the *Chapman*. It will continue by outlining the principal consequences of the drama for Governor Lachlan Macquarie. By returning the officers for trial on some of the most serious charges that can be brought before a court, the wayward governor, as he would have been regarded by some of his peers in London, had challenged the prevailing orthodoxy that never gave the benefit of the doubt to the convict. While it has not been possible to discover the next phase of Surgeon Dewar's career, using documents surviving from the East India Company we do have an insight into the medium-term life of Captain Drake. At least one convict who survived four months on the *Chapman* went on to make headlines several decades later, having established himself with confidence as a resident of his adopted home. The story of Peter Pidgeon ended up rivalling much of what transpired on his journey to the southern hemisphere. One of the places that the horrors of the *Chapman* went almost completely unnoticed was the Cove of Cork, where the voyage began. Life progressed as normal in the southern Irish port from where thousands more convicts would depart for New South Wales. This chapter will sketch the expansion of the transportation infrastructure, including the introduction of a permanently moored hulk in the early 1820s.

It has been claimed that the 1817 delivery of convicts to New South Wales on board the *Chapman* left a lasting stain on the colony. In 1954 the newspaper *Truth* reported that Macquarie had been vindicated by the Wentworth-Wylde-Campbell report and that it would be a long time before Sydney forgot the horrors visited upon it by that ship.[197] Whatever the truth of what happened during those four months, there is little doubt that no one on board the ship, whether above or below deck, will have forgotten the fear, the trauma and the bloodshed of the journey to the colony. For the prisoners who survived and were not returned to London as witnesses, there was little option but to concede to the reality of their new life in this strange new land. For the first part of that new life they were obliged to serve out the sentence that had brought them there in the first place.

The surviving convicts

Pardons were typically given to convicts who were serving life sentences and were one means of achieving freedom. A conditional pardon dictated that the convict was required to remain in New South Wales. An absolute pardon allowed them to stay or to return to Ireland or England. Governor Macquarie made active use of the pardon system, particularly for those convicts who had proven themselves worthy through good behaviour.[198] Appendix 5 lists some former *Chapman* convicts who were eventually granted pardons, but the number is likely to be much higher. A certificate of freedom was presented to the convict once they had completed their (usually) seven- or fourteen-year sentence of transportation. It was a declaration that the convict had served their sentence and was now free. Some convicts were sent to the colony on life sentences and could not receive a certificate of freedom, so instead they had to hope for a pardon. A list of *Chapman* convicts granted these certificates can be seen in Appendix 4. The ticket of leave was granted to a convict while they were still serving their sentence. It allowed them to work for their own benefit and to acquire property. Among the conditions were requirements to attend a muster every few months and to attend church on a weekly basis. The ticket could be renewed on an annual basis and the convict could marry or even bring members of their family to the colony. If the convict adhered to these conditions then they were relaxed as the sentence progressed. The key immovable condition of the ticket was that the individual remain in the colony until the full sentence was served. Appendix 6 provides another partial list of those granted a ticket from the 1817 voyage.

An 1812 select committee on transportation in Westminster outlined the process that dictated the release of prisoners from their sentence of transportation. Upon the expiration of their sentence, the convict was immediately considered to be free and they were confronted with two options: they were either free to return to their home country or stay in the colony. If they decided upon the latter option then they could take advantage of opportunities that would scarcely come their way in rural Ireland, or indeed England, during the early nineteenth century. A land grant of 40 acres was available to an unmarried man and this was increased if he was married and had children. Equipment and stock were made available to them and for eighteen months they were supplied from government stores. The governments in London and in the colony viewed this as an opportunity for the now liberated convict to become independent participants in a new society with all the incentives to good behaviour that came from immediate land ownership.[199] In reality, the scheme was far more about building a new modern civilisation in New South Wales based upon English norms and administrative methods. English and Irish convicts with their land grants were an essential part of that new civilisation.

Land grants were available not only to convicts who had served their sentences but also to those who were pardoned or emancipated by the sitting governor. The conditions were the same as for those who had completed their sentences but the notion of pardons was particularly troublesome for the 1812 select committee. The members felt that the system was open to abuse both by a governor and by the convicts. It was claimed that in certain years up to 150 pardons were granted, some of them when convicts had just arrived at the colony. Those who received the pardons rarely had to demonstrate any level of good conduct or 'exemplary behaviour'. A governor would curry favour with his population, many of whom were convicts or former convicts, with his liberal use of this mechanism.[200]

It was claimed that those who wished to leave the colony and return home had little difficulty in making this happen. All men, with the exception of 'the aged and infirm', would easily find work on ships similar to the ones that brought them there in the first place. This would allow them to work their passage home. The committee acknowledged that the options for women were considerably more limited, with most needing to resort to prostitution on the ships in order to secure the cost of their return.[201] In truth, for men or women who could not secure their passage back to Europe, that sentence handed down in a crowded courtroom in Cork, Belfast or Dublin was automatically converted to one of a lifetime in exile.

The reprimand of Governor Macquarie

The acquittal in London of every one of those charged in relation to the *Chapman* voyage is not, with the benefit of hindsight, a surprise. Had faster modes of communication been available, Macquarie would have been instructed by his superiors in government to desist from prosecuting or further investigating the officers and soldiers of the ship. He would likely have been directed to allow the ship to continue on the planned voyage to India following a cursory examination of the circumstances surrounding the deaths onboard. It is even possible that he might have been asked to consider criminal charges against some of the surviving convicts who were deemed to have been ringleaders of a mutiny. Those faster modes of communication were not available, however, so the government in London was forced to accept that the maverick governor was acting within his powers. Whether they agreed or not, it was within his remit to return a group of senior English naval officers and soldiers to face charges of the murder of and cruelty towards a cargo of Irish convicts. Macquarie likely knew that the charges would ultimately collapse but given the nature of his governorship of New South Wales it was obvious that he was trying to send a message about the treatment of convicts. The government was not interested in hearing any message.

In the immediate aftermath of the acquittals at the Admiralty Sessions, a number of Whitehall officials began shaping their planned response to the colonial government. Detailing the overall facts of the case, the Solicitor of the Treasury, Mr Maule, reported to Under-Secretary Hobhouse that those charged in the murders of the convicts had either been found not guilty or had not faced the full charges due to the absence of evidence. He pointed out that the convict witnesses who had received a royal pardon in order to return to London and testify for the prosecution were now at liberty and had returned to Ireland.[202] In a further exchange with another under-secretary, Hobhouse implored his colleague to call Lord Bathurst's attention to the 'public inconvenience' brought about by these trials. He lamented that thirteen Irish convicts – 'some of them of the worst description' – were now set free with royal pardons. Given that the offences alleged in the prosecutions occurred on the high seas, it was accepted that Governor Macquarie had no jurisdiction to try the cases in New South Wales. Nonetheless, it was worth reminding him that serious inconvenience was caused by organising such trials in England and should such unfortunate events present themselves in the future the accused should only be returned for prosecution if there was certainty that the evidence would stand up before a jury.[203]

Having received the contents of the Wentworth-Wylde-Campbell investigation many months earlier the officials in London would have been well aware that the decision to return Drake, Dewar and their colleagues for trial in London was very much Macquarie's alone. Those reports and the attendant chains of correspondence clearly demonstrated Wentworth and Wylde's reluctance to support a prosecution. To use modern parlance, the governor of New South Wales was on a solo run. In April 1819, in a letter from Downing Street, the Secretary for War and the Colonies, Earl Bathurst, outlined his displeasure to Macquarie. While he believed that such an unusual scenario was unlikely to present itself to the governor again, he castigated him for sending these individuals for trial in England without 'a body of evidence worthy of credit'.[204] Officialdom in early nineteenth-century London did not appreciate a solo run.

The fate of Captain John Drake

Prior to taking command of the *Chapman* in late 1816, John Drake worked in the service of the East India Company for approximately eleven years. His first voyage took place in 1804 and his last in 1815. During the course of six voyages he worked his way up from midshipman to second mate. During the fourth of these voyages, while working as third mate on the *Astell*, he witnessed action against two French frigates and a small warship known as a corvette. According to his own account of these encounters, the officers and crew earned great commendations not only from the Honourable Court of Directors (of the East India Company) but also from the Lords of the Admiralty. After his final voyage on the *Thames*, that ship was dismantled and his service with the company concluded.

At this point the owner of the *Thames*, Abel Chapman, had another vessel in the service of the company. That ship was hired to take convicts to New South Wales and so John Drake, after over a decade of service in lesser roles, became captain of the *Chapman*. This perhaps goes some way to explaining his lack of leadership, indecision and poor choices during the 1817 voyage to New South Wales. Not only was it his first voyage as a sea captain but he was also the chief gaoler of 200 Irish convicts. He was wholly under-experienced for such a challenge. He had never before been the overall commander of a transportation voyage where he was required to deal with a regular crew, a military regiment and a cargo of convicts. Added to this was the fact that this was possibly the longest voyage he had ever undertaken.

Recounting a summary of that voyage several decades later, he described how a mutiny among the convicts on board led to his own detention in England for two years. He claimed he was partly on trial and partly attempting to recover £1,000 in expenses from the government. It turned out that he prevailed in both endeavours. Around 1819 he lost a number of powerful friends, mostly because they died and not necessarily in relation to any scandal around the *Chapman*. He decided that he wanted to go back to the life he loved so much and return to the sea. He petitioned the East India Company for an appointment as a third mate but was unsuccessful. In 1820 a friend of his named Mr Templar secured £20,000 in financing for the construction of two ships for service within the company and he promised the command of one of those vessels to Drake. Templar did not fulfil his obligations, however, and the now-isolated Drake was once again disappointed.

Around this time another well-connected friend recommended to the East India Company that Drake be appointed to a position that had become vacant in Calcutta. This application was unsuccessful because the post had already been filled. As the 1820s continued, so too did the former captain's misfortune. In 1823 he and a number of friends tendered to build a 1,300-ton ship for the company but this was rejected and the project was permanently stalled. The following year, having also been unproductive in all his efforts to obtain a position as a chief or second mate – in his own words due to a surplus of qualified men – he undertook a voyage to the coast of Guinea. While it is not clear in what capacity he travelled or what was the purpose of the voyage, according to Drake himself it was unsuccessful. In 1826 the captain of the *Kellie Castle* offered him the position of chief mate but as the appointment was 'in the gift of the Honourable Hugh Lindsay', when Drake formally applied it had already been filled.

In 1827, with no sign of a return to the East India Company, he took command of the *City of Rochester*, a 500-ton ship owned by one of his friends. He spent the next two years sailing the Mediterranean before tendering the ship to the 'Honourable Company for Bengal', but this was rejected and the vessel sold. On the advice of friends, he once again waited for an opportunity to return to service with the East India Company. They counselled him that new ships would be required and that he, along with other out-of-work officers, would have a fair chance of an appointment.

By 1835, John Drake was clearly in dire economic straits and threw himself at the mercy of the East India Company. Here he was, a man with five children and no means of supporting them or himself – he did not mention a wife or mother of the children. He also supported an aged mother who raised five children while the family was in the service of the company. Three of his siblings died in India and another – presumably his brother John – was also a sea captain. In supporting an elderly parent he was now dependent on the charity of others and was himself suffering from a severe attack of fever. He was in receipt of assistance from his 'fellow brother officers' during his convalescence.

In what must have been a humiliating climb-down from those heady days as the commander of the *Chapman* where he exercised so much authority, albeit badly, Drake effectively begged the company for employment. He was willing to work in any capacity in which they saw him fit to serve. Failing this he implored the 'honourable court to place me out of the reach of the want of bread' by granting him a pension. Ironically, Drake's petition was accompanied by a handwritten positive reference from Abel Chapman. He confirmed that Drake had been of service on his vessels during the seasons 1811–12 and 1813–14 as a second officer. The letter also confirmed that Drake commanded the *Chapman* on a voyage to New South Wales and India beginning in 1816 and ending in 1818.[205]

John Drake was granted some sort of pension allowance from the East India Company, though the figure is not available. In the absence of further documentary evidence, it is impossible to fully account for his misfortunes in the decades following the ill-fated voyage of the *Chapman*. It is possible that he became somewhat of a pariah in the upper echelons of the shipping industry, whether among the Admiralty or the East India Company. Likewise, it is possible that he was a victim of the diminishing influence of the company both in political and commercial terms.

The crime and punishment of Peter Pidgeon

The *Chapman* delivered its convict cargo in the midst of an extraordinary social engineering process that was designed not only to solve an overcrowding problem in England and Irish prisons, but also to construct a new modern society in the farthest-flung colony of the empire. It was inevitable that those convicts would make their mark on the colony, something that was, after all, the intention of the original settlers. Convicts were necessary to settle upon, build and expand new communities from nothing. Free settlers would soon follow and it was inevitable, as with any society, that the combination of law-abiding and potentially unruly inhabitants would bring with it many of the same social problems that they left behind in Europe. It is impossible to trace the path of every convict who survived the 1817 voyage from Ireland. There was likely an evolving pattern across the entire transportation period where some convicts will have continued in crime, some will have met with tragedy, others are known to have acquired wealth, while the majority probably received land grants and faded into the historical tapestry that wove the creation of modern Australia.

One *Chapman* convict in particular is known to have made his mark on the history of his adopted land – for all the wrong reasons. Peter Pidgeon was twenty-four years old and from Queen's County when he was convicted of having concealed arms in 1816.[206] Sentenced to seven years' transportation, his journey to New South Wales appears to have been uneventful. He was not involved in any of the skirmishes that marked the voyage and it is not noted that he was wounded or found himself in the sickbay at any point during the journey. Yet, thirty years after being deposited in Port Jackson under a sentence of transportation, Peter Pidgeon caused a sensation when he faced the wrath of another court.

On Thursday, 15 April 1847, Pidgeon appeared before magistrates in East Maitland, where he was questioned under suspicion of the murder of William Taylor of Illawarra. Many years earlier Taylor drove a mail coach between Singleton and Maitland but in recent times had settled in Illawarra, where he owned a cart, two horses and a small property. He survived by selling fish using his horse and cart. Taylor was known by the nickname 'Coachey' and was described as small in stature. Peter Pidgeon was also well known in Illawarra and worked there as a farm labourer up to two and a half years earlier, when he relocated to the Maitland district. He returned yet again to Illawarra where, claiming to be ill, he managed to persuade a local farmer named Waters to allow him to live on his property, where he did odd jobs in exchange for food.

While back in Illawarra he renewed an acquaintance with William Taylor. He persuaded Taylor to take his horses and cart to join him in taking coal to Morpeth. The pair left Illawarra around June 1846 but Pidgeon did not tell his host, Mr Waters, that he was leaving with Taylor, giving him to understand he was making the journey alone. Upon reaching the Wollombi the two men stopped on the Great Northern Road from Sydney, where they stayed one night with a farmer named Medhurst. Further along their journey they stopped at McDougall's public house for an hour and a half to water their horses. The proprietor and Taylor were somewhat acquainted from Taylor's days on the mail coach. McDougall tried to persuade Taylor to sell him his shaft-horse but was declined on the basis that the animal provided a key contributon to his livelihood back in Maitland. The two men once again took to the road – it was the last time that Taylor was seen alive.

The next sighting of Peter Pidgeon came at the property of a farmer named Minalow, about 7 or 8 miles from East Maitland. He had known the farmer for approximately twelve years and turned up during the month of June with a cart and two horses but no companion. Pidgeon told Minalow that he bought the horses at Wollongong and asked to leave them at his property for a day or two until he arranged longer-term accommodation. He subsequently left just one animal with his old friend and came back frequently to check the other, which he retrieved after three weeks. It later emerged that he sold one of the animals to a man named Michael Downey on 13 July. After leaving Minalow's, Pidgeon moved on to West Maitland, where he spent the night in the lodging house of yet another acquaintance. He told John Maher that he had purchased the horse that same day in Maitland for £13. Maher was taken aback by this claim because he had always found Pidgeon to be unreliable and unable to settle his debts when he previously lodged at his house.

Leaving Maitland, the Irishman headed back toward Illawarra, where he was spotted by the farmer, Medhurst. Expressing surprise that he was leaving Maitland and travelling alone, Pidgeon implied that he had been unable to do much business there. Medhurst specifically enquired about Pidgeon's former travelling companion, only to be told that Taylor was making the journey by water and they would meet at the other side of the country. On returning to Illawarra he sought a loan of £2 from Waters to allow him to buy Taylor's horse and cart, which he claimed to have left behind at Maitland. Waters duly obliged and Pidgeon disappeared, only to return a fortnight later with a horse and cart. When he was asked by Waters what Taylor would now do to earn a living, Pidgeon claimed he was buying a light cart and would work with his other horse.

After much to-ing and fro-ing between Maitland and Illawarra, those familiar with Pidgeon became suspicious of his transactions with the horses and cart, his stories about the now-absent Taylor, and his conflicting accounts of his travels. Magistrates in Wollongong, in communication with their counterparts in Maitland, became interested in his activities and questioned him on the possession of his property. With nothing found against him he was permitted to continue his travels. This was late February 1847. It had emerged that a body, now known to be that of William Taylor, was found in East Maitland the previous October. His former acquaintances had now become so suspicious of Pidgeon's behaviour that some of them, notably Maher, refused to allow him to stay on their property.

Preliminary judicial examinations at Wollongong and Maitland led to the issuing of a warrant for the arrest of Pidgeon after items of clothing belonging to Taylor were found in his room. On 17 March he was taken into custody by the farmer Waters when he arrived at his property. Waters handed the elusive former labourer over to the police, where he made a number of statements about the horses, the clothing and other property. Peter Pidgeon, having spent decades as a free man since the expiration of the sentence that brought him to Australia on the *Chapman*, would never know liberty again.

Meanwhile, the body of William Taylor was in a state of decomposition by the time it was discovered and identification was only confirmed after a number of acquaintances had the unpleasant task of examining the remains. A married woman named Harriet Orphan from Illawarra had washed, mended and kept house for Taylor for many years. She was able to identify items of clothing, including some that she herself had repaired. She also confirmed that the skull and remaining hair were that of her former sometime-employer. Two other men familiar with Taylor confirmed that the skull was that of Taylor, although they could not agree whether he had two teeth missing from his upper jaw or his lower jaw. The public house owner McDougall also confirmed that the clothing was identical to that worn by Taylor the night he and Pidgeon spent at his property.[207]

The case came to court on Wednesday, 15 September 1847, when Peter Pidgeon was indicted for the murder of William 'Coachey' Taylor. The murder was alleged to have taken place on 1 September of the previous year at Maitland and the first count stated that Pidgeon assaulted the victim with a blunt instrument, wounding him on the left side of the head and on the stomach, back and sides. William Taylor died instantly. The second count claimed that the assault took place by throwing the victim on the ground, where he was struck and beaten by Pidgeon's hands and feet. In the third count it was stated that the assault was committed with the assailants' hands and feet. The final count repeated that hands and feet were used to cast Taylor to the ground.

In court, the Solicitor General pointed out that the date of 1 September was not necessarily strictly accurate but was put forward as a probability. The first indictment was, he argued, where the greatest weight of evidence rested against Peter Pidgeon and the subsequent three were of little value. The first point for the jury to agree was that the body was that of William Taylor, as claimed by the police and their witnesses. Once this was agreed then they must turn their attention to the theft by the accused of the possessions of William Taylor because this was surely a key indicator of guilt. Against defence objections, the judge allowed this line of argument to go before the jury and so began the questioning of witnesses.

Archibald Osborne was a magistrate in Illawarra and was aware of William 'Coachey' Taylor when he was alive. He was also familiar with his horses and cart. He testified that the accused turned up at the police office at Wollongong on about 3 or 4 March of that year wishing to account for his possession of the horses and cart belonging to the dead man. At the time, Pidgeon claimed he purchased them from Taylor at a small public house near Yeoman's Hotel at Maitland for £13. A man named Hines witnessed the sale. He promised to produce either Hines or Coachey Taylor to satisfy the magistrate but this never transpired. Once the magistrates in Illawarra communicated with the police in Maitland a warrant was issued for the arrest of Pidgeon.

John Waters, who hosted the accused at his farm near Wollongong, was next to testify and confirmed that Pidgeon stayed with him on and off for about six weeks. When he returned he wanted to borrow £2 towards Taylor's horse and cart, which he claimed to have purchased for £13. He went on to repeat much of the evidence about Pidgeon's movements as they were previously stated during the committal hearings five months earlier following his arrest.

The chief constable of Wollongong, Thomas Fowler, testified that he knew both the accused and the victim in this case. He was also familiar with Taylor's horses and the cart, which were central to the case against Peter Pidgeon. On 11 March last he took a warrant to the Waters house to arrest Pidgeon but the Irishman was missing. The following day he returned and, prompted by Waters, he removed the cart and some boxes which apparently contained clothing and other items owned by Taylor. A Maitland resident named Jane McDermott described how she was gathering material to make brooms at the back of a local burial ground when she found herself standing beside a human head. It was lying among some thorny scrub with no apparent attempt to conceal it from public view. Having become ill at the sight of the head she was unable to report it to police for two days.

Chief Constable George Wood of Maitland described accompanying the distraught woman to the site where she found the head. The remainder of the body was in a skeletal state and lying face downwards, with the hands turned up behind. The remnants of clothing were obvious and tufts of hair remained about the neck and head. The body was that of a smallish man – which fitted the stature of Taylor – with small hands and feet. An inquest led by a Dr Alfred Eyde was held and the remains were buried, only to be later exhumed. The back of the skull showed evidence of a large fracture. Dr Eyde testified that the remains had been lying in the same location for somewhere between six and eight weeks. After giving a detailed account of the possible physical appearance of the victim in life, he concluded that death was probably instant, the result of a blow from a heavy blunt instrument.

Harriet Orphan once again testified as to the identity of William Taylor. She gave evidence of a conversation between him and Pidgeon where the defendant tried to persuade him to believe he had a cart at Maitland earning seven shillings per day carrying coal to a steamer. He implored him to join in the enterprise by bringing over his own two horses and cart. Once they left, Harriet never heard from Taylor again; though he typically wrote to her when he was away, they had no further communication. As she had spent years tending to his clothing, she provided detailed, almost expert, testimony on his attire and how it matched that of the body found at Maitland, as well as the items taken from the house of John Waters.

Several further witnesses were questioned about their encounters with Peter Pidgeon during the summer months of 1846. They included William Medhurst, John Maher and John McDougall. During the early sightings he was accompanied by William Taylor but subsequently only turned up alone. The prosecution was particularly thorough, drawing evidence from multiple sources on matters such as ownership of the horses and cart, the identity of the box found at the Waters property, as well as the clothing worn by the corpse discovered at Maitland.

Proceedings adjourned at 8.30 p.m. on the first evening in court with the jury placed under the charge of the sheriff for the night. The next day, many of those originally questioned were recalled to the witness stand to corroborate or reinforce testimony given during the first day of the trial. When the defence counsel – Mr Purefoy – stood up to address the jury on behalf of his client he declared that this was one of the most mysterious cases with which he had ever been confronted. It was true, he agreed, that there were several facts that pointed directly towards Peter Pidgeon's guilt as the murderer of William Taylor. There were many more details, however, that proved totally inconsistent with the notion of guilt. The defender pointed out that the presumption of guilt very much depended on the notion that his client was guilty of the theft of the victim's belongings. The problem with this was that Pidgeon was not charged with stealing from William Taylor, either before or after his violent death. He argued that the evidence of a murder, let alone one committed by Pidgeon, was purely circumstantial.

It appears that the defence called just one witness and in doing so they introduced an explosive racial element into the case. John Luke testified that the Maitland races took place between 12 and 20 August in 1846 and he was familiar with the location where the body was found. On the first day of the races he was walking through the bush towards Morpeth and about a quarter of a mile from the spot where the body was eventually found when he met 'a black fellow' who seemed particularly gruff. The 'black', as he was described in court, walked up a gully close to the place where the body of William Taylor would later be found. He met with three men of his own race and together they spoke in their own language. The men were sitting by a fire cleaning their spears. A few moments later the four natives rose and took off in the direction of a quarry, from where John Luke could hear 'a great shouting'. Following some distance back, he saw twenty or thirty native men, all armed and all shouting.

Joined by the first four men, the larger group again moved off towards a larger body of natives that numbered close to 200. As John Luke approached the group he was confronted by 'a strange black' who asked him what he wanted. He identified himself as being from Morpeth and told the native man he wanted a spear. The spear never material-ised and Luke testified that he had never found the natives to exhibit such an unfriendly demeanour upon being approached by white people. The body of William Taylor would later be found 50 or 60 yards from the quarry, from the very spot where this group of 200 native men was gathered. To this line of questioning the prosecutor countered that the circumstances described by John Luke were akin to some form of native tribal ceremony or ritual rather than anything more sinister.[208] The intro-duction of this incident was either a last-ditch effort exploiting the white suspicion of natives and thus designed to give the jury cause for doubt, or a genuine series of encounters. Either way, it was impossible for the jury to see through the fog and no corroborating witness to this evidence was offered.

At the end of this testimony the judge summed up the case to the jury. He emphasised the horror of the crime of which James Pidgeon was accused. There were three overall points on which they should come to agreement. William Taylor was dead. He died as a result of murder. That murder was committed by Peter Pidgeon. There were no mitigating circumstances and the jury should come up with a verdict of either guilty or non-guilty. If they decided, however, that there were some mitigating circumstances then they could find him guilty of manslaughter. He admitted that there was no direct evidence of the crime and the jury would need to weigh the facts very closely before they found the prisoner guilty. They must be clear that Pidgeon committed the crime with his own hands and to the exclusion of any other perpetrator. With those words the jury retired to consider the case against Peter Pidgeon.

Clearly the jury felt confident that they were sufficiently acquainted with the two days of testimony because just thirty minutes later they returned a verdict of guilty against Peter Pidgeon on count one. Murder. The remaining counts did not matter. Pidgeon was remanded in custody to await sentencing for the murder of William 'Coachey' Taylor. One onlooker pointed out that 'throughout his long trial the prisoner preserved a quiet demeanour, betraying no emotion, yet without appearing indifferent'.[209] In late September he returned to court for sentencing. The outcome was all but inevitable and the court made clear that no pleas for mercy would be entertained. Peter Pidgeon was sentenced to death.[210]

On Thursday, 4 November 1847 the guilty prisoner was brought to the place of execution at Newcastle. A jury at the Maitland Circuit Court had found him guilty of the wilful murder of William 'Coachey' Taylor at Morpeth. The Reverend Mr Dowling of Newcastle attended to Pidgeon's spiritual needs during those crucial moments. The process was supervised by the Under-Sheriff, Mr Prout. The Reverend Dowling announced that he had been asked by the condemned man to acknowledge that his sentence was just, that he was indeed guilty of the crime for which he had been condemned to this fate. He asked for the prayers of the assembled gathering in those final moments. It was reported that since the day the guilty verdict was pronounced, the convicted man had 'attended most assiduously to the intrusions of his spiritual director, and appeared to be fully impressed with his awful situation'.[211] Without much hesitation the lever was pulled and the journey that Peter Pidgeon began from the Cove of Cork in March 1817 on the *Chapman* convict ship finally came to an end. While it has not been possible to ascertain the fate of every convict on that voyage, it is believed that Pidgeon's was probably the most devastating of all the survivors.

The Cove of Cork after the Chapman

The best estimate suggests that the *Chapman* was the nineteenth convict transport to leave the Cove of Cork for New South Wales. Bateson's *The Convict Ships* provides a comprehensive list of vessels that departed Ireland and England during the entire transportation period. The first to leave Ireland and Cork was the *Queen* in 1791. That ship carried 133 male convicts and twenty-two females; there were seven deaths. The process continued only slowly during the remainder of the decade. Challenging what may be a broader popular understanding of transportation as a large-scale form of punishment, the reality was that just six other convict sailings left Ireland during the 1790s and all of those were from Cork. Two ships left in 1793, one each in 1795 and 1796, and two in 1799. This will have heightened the sense of occasion that was the departure of such a vessel from the port. Given that the sailings were so rare, there would not necessarily have been a streamlined system of processing prisoners.

The first nineteenth-century sailing to leave was *Anne I* in 1800, carrying 147 men and twenty-four women. The process accelerated very slightly from then onwards. Two ships each left in 1801 and 1802; the two that left in 1801 were noted as having left from 'Ireland' rather than Cork. Two more left in 1805 and another two in 1809. The pace picked up considerably during the second decade of the century, with twenty-one shiploads of convicts banished to the colony. One of these was the *Chapman*. Again, four of these were noted as having left 'Ireland' rather than Cork. The single busiest year was 1819, with seven vessels leaving Cork. On these seven ships were 802 male and 226 female prisoners. A golden age of transportation from Ireland took hold with a total of fifty-one sailings from Dublin and Cork during the 1820s. Eleven of those ships sailed from Dublin and one from 'Ireland'. The 1830s saw the growth of that golden age with sixty-one sailings, but with a notable decline from Cork towards the end of the decade. Around twenty-six ships left from Dublin, two from 'Ireland' and the remainder from Cork. According to the data produced by Bateson, no ship left Cork for New South Wales after the *Diamond* exiled 162 female convicts in 1837. During the 1840s just five ships left Ireland and all sailed from Dublin. It was nine years before the next and final ship departed.[212]

The one feature that marked the exile of Irish people to New South Wales from the first sailing to the last was the gender imbalance that existed. On the seven ships that left Cork between 1791 and 1799, there were 973 men and 232 women. During the first decade of the nineteenth century some 1,043 men and 330 women were banished. Between 1810 and 1819 the number increased in line with the amount of sailings. This period saw 2,564 men and 623 women, a continuation of the broad gender gap. With the 1820s came that explosion of the use of transportation as a punishment option. An astonishing 7,405 men and 1,311 women were ejected from their homeland. The numbers peaked with 9,042 men and 2,059 women sent during the 1830s, falling dramatically to 700 men and 252 women in the 1840s.[213]

A factor that may have contributed to the acceleration of transportation during the 1820s was the introduction of a convict hulk in Cork harbour around 1823. The inspector-general of prisons announced the development that same year. The intention was to use the stationary vessel for the warehousing of those sentenced to transportation at the various assizes around Ireland after the spring and summer sessions. He suggested that the convicts could be marched to Cork on foot as it would relieve the financial burden on the system. It was also hoped that the presence of the hulk would allow for the storing of greater numbers of prisoners in Cork, freeing up the gaols of the country and also allowing for their speedier removal to New South Wales.[214] The system of processing convicts that was absent at the beginning of the 1790s and well into the 1800s was now well and truly taking shape.

A year later the inspector reported that the hulk *Surprize* was operational and receiving convicts in Cork. In fact, the vessel received around 900 souls during that first year and was set up to facilitate up to 350 at one time. The vessel was praised for the state of its accommodation, diet, cleanliness and general regulations. The officers were also praised and a recommendation was put forward that a schoolmaster should be provided. Within this came the revelation that the convicts generally remained on the hulk for only a short period before transportation. Nonetheless, because almost all came from the local gaols of Ireland, they had been exposed to some form of learning and it would be useful to build on this during their final waiting period. Several prisoners were employed on board at carpentry, dressmaking and repair, as well as an age-old prison occupation, oakum picking.[215] It is worth remembering that the inspectors-general were always likely to put forward the most positive account of the hulk in Cork because this was essentially an initiative that the government needed to succeed in order to free up the local gaols and bolster the transportation system.

In 1826 the inspector continued to acclaim introduction of the *Surprize* as a mechanism to streamline the exile criminals from Ireland. It appears that the hulk and the convict depot, situated in an old barracks, somehow experienced a degree of overcrowding during the year prior to the report. This seems to have been caused by an enthusiasm at local level around the country to transfer prisoners for transportation to their holding locations in Cork as soon as possible. By the time this report was published the logjam was relieved by an exodus of convicts to New South Wales. The inspector repeated his praise for the operation of the hulk in Cork and again implored the authorities at local level to try and find some type of occupation for those on the vessel awaiting transportation.[216]

At the end of the 1820s the hulk was established as a key element of the transportation infrastructure in Cork. In 1829 the inspector found 257 prisoners on board and recommended that it would be preferable that the vessel be emptied for transportation before the assizes began sending more occupants for the limited onboard space. Approximately eighty individuals were occupied in tailoring, shoemaking, oakum picking and net-making, while a makeshift school was operated by three prisoners deemed capable of teaching.[217] The emphasis on ensuring that the convicts were occupied insofar as resources allowed was one that had already taken hold in the wider prison system and came to be a fundamental element of future reform efforts, particularly during the early twentieth century.

The best available population figures for the *Surprize* come in a medical officer report in 1834 outlining some financial and other data for that hulk and the *Essex* off Dublin. Between 1823 and the end of 1834 a total of 5,968 men and women occupied the *Surprize* in Cork. This led to a daily average of 148. There was just one recorded escape during the period; forty-three prisoners died from some form of disease or old age while one lost their life in a disturbance. Nine convicts succumbed to fever, eight died from 'debility and old age', seven from symptoms of consumption and seven from dysentery. Lower numbers of convicts died from conditions including dropsy, chest problems and erysipelas.[218] Whether it was a reflection of the state of convicts arriving at the hulk or the conditions inside the vessel, there is no question that the *Surprize* was a very unhealthy place.

The inspectors-general for the prisons of Ireland appeared keen to point out the sanitary conditions on board the *Surprize*. Each year they paid tribute to the airy conditions, the scrubbed floors and decks, and the general purity of the hulk. The 1835 figures, however, show that 5,753 convicts experienced some form of what the medical officer classified as 'disease'. Naturally there is likely to have been some overlap with some prisoners perhaps experiencing multiple conditions, meaning that there may have been many more fully healthy prisoners boarding the *Surprize* than the figures indicate. The most common medical condition was itch, experienced by 1,240 men and women. Catarrhal affections touched 763 of those on board, while 747 suffered some type of bowel affliction. The next highest disease was named as 'feverish cold', affecting 560 convicts, followed by 392 with 'cough'. Smaller numbers of prisoners presented with a wide variety of other illnesses including cholic [*sic*], venereal disease, consumption symptoms, swollen testicles, fever, scald head, herpetic eruption, rheumatism, jaundice, piles and 'idiotism'.[219]

One account of life on board the hulk in Cork was published in 1835. An unknown English convict found himself in the unfortunate situation of spending time on a number of hulks and at least two structurally unsound convict ships before eventually finding himself on the *Surprize*. The government was attempting to transport him and his fellow prisoners to Van Diemen's Land but thanks to an unfortunate series of mishaps they ended up spending a number of weeks on the hulk in Cork. The convict described his experience in harrowing detail:

> After the cholera had ceased, myself and seventeen other unfortunate companions were left in Cork harbour, mere skeletons, at a place called Harboling (Haulbowline). After being there some time we were put on board a hulk called the Surprise, where, if possible, we were obliged to suffer more in mind than we had before in body; for, added to filth, hunger and all manner of wretchedness, through our being Protestants, we were subject to great misery, most on board being Irish and Papists. They were used to cut our hammocks down at night, sticking awls through the bottoms of the hammocks into our bodies, and would have thought nothing of murdering us but for fear of the law. Through this treatment I was again taken ill, and continued so for three months; we were put into a small place called a chapel, between decks, and the captain allowed us to take air one hour at night.[220]

The man claimed that the Irish prisoners who had been tormenting these temporary refugee English convicts attempted to set fire to the *Surprize*. Eventually the captain decided that it was best to move the Englishmen elsewhere. With the decline in transportation, particularly from Cork harbour, the demand for the services of the *Surprize* also faded and by 1837 the vessel was decommissioned as a hulk and sold.

★

Whatever became of the much-brutalised William Leo? Did the sailors Nelson and Crawley continue onward with the *Chapman* from New South Wales and India? John Ennis and Peter Allen, who encountered the constable of the night watch in Bishop Street several years earlier, safely disembarked from the ship in July 1817. What future unfolded for them? Patrick Smith was the 'medical convict' and doctor's mate who was pardoned and returned to Europe, where he testified against the crew members at the Old Bailey. A significant historical figure in his own right, what happened to him once the final 'not guilty' verdict was declared at that trial? What was the fate of his superior on the *Chapman*, the incompetent Surgeon-Superintendent Alexander Dewar? So many of the figures that brought the story of that devastating journey to life have melted into history. Despite the best efforts of research, they have not revealed themselves, but this is not to say that they will not do so at some point in the future.

Perhaps the most important question of all is what happened to the *Chapman*? Two further convict transportation journeys to Australia awaited the now ageing vessel. In July 1824, almost seven years to the day after arriving with a prison filled with emaciated convicts in Port Jackson, the ship arrived in Hobart, Van Diemen's Land.[221] In late October 1826, this time carrying fewer convicts, the *Chapman* arrived once more at Hobart. The commander, Captain Millbank, deposited ninety-eight male prisoners, one officer and twenty privates. From there the ship took eleven convicts and some fourteen military personnel to New South Wales. The *Chapman* arrived back in Sydney on 4 November 1826 and it would be her final arrival in Australia as a convict vessel.[222] The future of the ship beyond this point is somewhat patchy with some voyages to Canada, North America and Africa. It is likely that she was decommissioned around 1854.

8

Conclusion

With its human cargo and full complement of supplies on board and ready to sail, the *Chapman* departed from Cobh on 15 March 1817. This is one of the few uncontested facts about the voyage. Three known versions of the voyage exist. One was offered by senior officers of the *Chapman*, another on behalf of the convicts, and a third in official correspondence from New South Wales to Dublin. The first two stemmed from separate judicial exercises, one of which was a full-scale trial for murder. After the vessel docked in Sydney in July and the authorities realised the scale of the mayhem that marked the voyage, the governor of New South Wales, Lachlan Macquarie, ordered a judge-led committee to investigate the events. It is the evidence presented to this inquiry that outlined the captain and his senior officers' perspectives. As a result of this proceeding, Macquarie ordered the captain and surgeon back to London, where they went on trial for murder. The principal evidence presented at that trial came from convict witnesses appearing for the prosecution.

One convict on the ship would go on to become a minor historical figure in his own right but not for any reason related to the killing and punishment that blighted the voyage. In chapter two we met Patrick Smith, a Tyrone-based 'white-collar criminal', when he was appointed doctor's mate on the *Chapman*. When he was marched into the sickbay that morning, Smith became a medical convict. In the *British Medical Journal* 160 years later, Smith was singled out as one of 'a small band of men who came not freely but as transportees' and went on to play an important role in the expansion of the medical profession in New South Wales.[223] Richards highlighted the importance of medical convicts, most of whom appeared to be male, during the early decades of the convicts. Eleven medical convicts travelled to New South Wales on the First Fleet and one of them, John Irving, was a convict. Smith was not the first Irish medical convict to land in the colony. Bryan O'Connor was transported for his role in the 1798 Rebellion in Ireland and arrived in Sydney from Cork in January 1800. He received a pardon in 1801 and this allowed him to practice medicine.[224] It is not known what, if any, background Patrick Smith may have had in medicine. Why Dewar was motivated to select him above all the other inmates to be his second-in-command in the sickbay is not at all clear. It may have been the non-violent nature of his criminality or it may simply have been based on intelligence gleaned from observation. In any event, Smith had no usefulness to the colony because he was one of those returned to London with a royal pardon in December 1817 to testify against the very surgeon-superintendent who had promoted him to a key position during the voyage.

According to the ship's captain, John Drake, suspicions were raised after just a week at sea. In evidence to the Wentworth inquiry, he claimed that whispers had been heard among the convicts to the effect that 'there's time enough yet' and 'the soldiers are good for nothing'.[225] It is not clear exactly whom is supposed to have heard these comments and how widespread they were. Nor do we know the specific context in which they were uttered. Captain Drake admitted that the number of physical punishments was increased after this time as the cat-o'-nine-tails was used in response to insolence and other minor breaches of discipline.[226] The French writer Charles Vidil described life on board a ship as offering a most appropriate space in which to generate mental turmoil, deception and insinuation.[227] Whether true or false, in proposing that conspiratorial mutterings were rife among the prisoners, Drake was sowing the seed of a defence that claimed he and his crew had reason for concern from early on in the voyage.

One of the key lines of defence offered by Drake and his officers around the cause of the problems on the voyage centre on supposed allegations from an inmate named Michael Collins. Sentenced to seven years' transportation for stealing money, Collins was twenty-six years old and from the town of Bandon in County Cork.[228] His motives are not clear but he is present in both versions of the chaos that marked the voyage. According to Drake, on the morning of 16 April Collins approached Third Mate Baxter who, upon hearing his story, rushed him to the captain's quarters. He claimed that a plot was being hatched below deck that would see the convicts break out of the prison, take over the crew's quarters and commandeer the vessel. They intended to murder the entire crew with the exception of the First Mate, who would be necessary to navigate the *Chapman* to America. He alleged that the convicts had been told by the ringleaders that anyone who resisted would be smothered with their own blankets, cut into pieces and their body parts ejected from the ship through the portholes. The three prisoners he alleged to be the chief plotters were William Leo, Francis Murphy and Peter Allan. They intended to 'butcher' the ship's officers, put on their clothing and assume the appearance of official members of the crew. In the event that any passing vessel should become suspicious, they would place 100 prisoners in irons above deck to avoid suspicion. Finally, the plotters, according to Collins, had even gone so far as to draw up a menu for the celebratory meal that would happen once the mutiny was complete. This feast was to include roast turkey, pigs, brandy, port and Madeira wine.[229] At Captain Drake's trial before the Admiralty Sessions in London in January 1819, it emerged that Collins had stated that the convicts were all forced to swear an oath to take the ship.[230]

This account becomes confused for a number of reasons. Firstly, Collins is alleged to have made these claims; the extent to which they were fabricated or embellished by the senior crew has to be drawn into question. Secondly, even if Collins did make the allegations exactly as outlined, he may have had any number of reasons to lie and the captain and his officers do not seem to have tested the claims to any extent. Thirdly, five months after the *Chapman* docked in Sydney, a letter from a government official in New South Wales to counterparts in Dublin described 'two villainous prisoners giving private (false) representations to the Captain and Doctor'.[231] The surviving convicts made no mention of a second alleged informant to the Wentworth inquiry but described Collins as a 'sneaking rogue' who had hoped to earn a free pardon by providing false information.[232] If this particular allegation was true then Michael Collins was guilty of provoking one of the bloodiest episodes on board any vessel during the transportation era.

The violence on the *Chapman* took place as a result of two incidents about ten days apart. The two official accounts of the voyage agree that nothing significant occurred after departing Cork until the night of 17 April, incidentally one day after Collins was alleged to have notified the captain of the 'plot'. At the January 1819 trial in London this initial episode was described as 'a melancholy conflict between the commander of the vessel and the convicts, under the supposition of an insurrection on the part of the convicts'.[233] The officers' version of the first salvos outlined how the cook noticed the forward hatch being forced up and raised the alarm. Captain Drake was drunk in his cabin – an apparently common occurrence. Third Mate Baxter and Lieutenant Busteed – both of whom feature heavily in all versions of the events – rushed on deck and ordered the soldiers and crew to take up arms because a 'tumult' had broken out in the prison. Gunfire was rained against the closed doors of the prison for about ten minutes. Baxter claimed he called on the 'mutineers' to surrender but received no response. Eventually cries for 'mercy' were heard among the screams of the wounded. Neither Captain Drake nor Surgeon Dewar would enter the prison quarters until the next morning, where they subsequently discovered two dead convicts and six 'mortally hurt'. It was noted that 'the brains of one lay scattered about his bed'.[234]

The convict population's interpretation of this event differs significantly. Part of it came from Terence Kiernan, a twenty-seven-year-old trainee clergyman from County Louth. Kiernan was convicted of the 'felony of bank notes' in July 1816 in Drogheda and sentenced to transportation for seven years.[235] He claimed that on the evening of 17 April, Third Mate Baxter appeared in the hatchway wielding a cutlass and bellowing abuse at the prisoners. Within minutes a volley of musket-fire was directed into the prison quarters and Kiernan claims that Baxter shouted 'fire away boys, kill every one of them'. Ignoring hysterical appeals from the cowering prisoners, the firing continued for a half hour. Once it ceased, a number of the wounded, who lay naked and lacking water, died during the night, which was marked below deck by overpowering heat. The one point upon which Kiernan agreed with the testimony of the officers in the retelling of this part of the events is that neither the captain nor the surgeon would enter the prison that night.[236]

That the events of the night of 17 April are strongly contested by both versions is hardly surprising. The two sides needed to protect their respective positions and both would have been keenly aware of the possibility of criminal prosecution arising from the affair. The aftermath of that night seems, however, to be less contested. During the days immediately following that night, two of the alleged munity ringleaders were subjected to 'ferocious punishments'. Baxter, who by all accounts was one of the more brutal of the senior officers on board, grabbed a whip from the bosun's mate, who was apparently preparing to administer a punishment.[237] The December 1817 account from within the New South Wales government concurs with this version and claims that Baxter grabbed the whip because he believed the bosun's mater (or Boatswain) would not have delivered a sufficiently severe flogging. To prevent further insubordination, he ordered fourteen prisoners to be double-ironed handcuffed and chained on the poop deck for the remainder of the voyage. A chain cable was run between their legs and if one of them made 'the least movement' they were to be flogged. Likewise, if they 'made water between the decks' they were also to be flogged for uncleanliness. This, allegedly, was a regular occurrence.[238] While these attempted deterrents would not have been unusual, in the case of the *Chapman* they appear to have been severe.

One of the grim punishment highlights of this part of the voyage took place when three of the prisoners – possibly the three originally named as ringleaders by Collins – were brought up on deck, where they were to be shot.[239] They were ordered to pray for their souls before being granted a reprieve by Baxter. In exchange for their lives they were punished with forty lashes each. Following a flogging, one of the alleged ringleaders – William Leo – was tied to the main yard-arm, thrown overboard and dragged along behind the ship until he was nearly dead. Upon his return to the ship the officers chained him to the deck and applied salt to the wounds without any surgical supervision, while the surgeon refused him medical attention.[240] While many of the prisoners were apparently paying a heavy physical price for the events of 17 April, this was not sufficient to prevent another serious disturbance on the *Chapman*.

Convict mortality

The high level of convict mortality on the 1817 voyage of the *Chapman* could be set aside as something of an aberration when compared with most other convict transports. McDonald and Shlomowitz point to two distinct homogeneous periods during the transportation era. The first was 1788–1814 and was noted for inadequate health screening and mediocre hygiene standards. This led to higher death rates. The second period was 1815–1868 and saw better screening and hygiene, and notably lower death rates.[241] The flaws in the early period were partly accounted for by the lack of authority vested in the surgeon. While he did oversee the embarkations of convicts and monitored each one for infectious diseases, he was quite often overruled by ship masters or owners, who enjoyed a financial benefit from delivering the maximum number of convicts, no matter what their condition. With the introduction of the term 'surgeon-superintendent' from around 1815, the medical officer had greater authority and enjoyed full control over the convicts.[242] With no epidemic voyages after 1814, McDonald and Shlomowitz point out that the main factor threatening the lives of those on a convict ship was the length of the voyage itself.[243] The death toll accrued on the *Chapman* was, therefore, an anomaly. It was claimed by the officers at the end of the voyage that just one individual died as a result of an infectious disease. In an almost self-congratulatory debrief it was seen as somewhat of a badge of honour that all the other deaths were the result of gunfire. The situation below deck on the average convict ship was typically atrocious, although measures including fumigation were used to keep the prisoners alive. As well as lower mortality rates, the health record on the nineteenth-century ships was also better than the earlier convict and emigrant vessels.[244] In reality, it transpired that the men transported on the *Chapman* faced a far greater threat than any eighteenth-century naval disease.

Between 1810 and 1816, a total of 117 convicts died during their voyage to New South Wales. This was across nineteen voyages that originally embarked 3,377 convicts. The highest number of casualties occurred on board the *General Hewitt*, with thirty-four deaths out of 300 embarkations. The second highest was on the *Surrey*, with thirty-six deceased out of 200 convicts. Finally, ten convicts out of 220 lost their lives during the passage of the *Three Bees*.[245] Mortality rates on each of the other seventeen voyages were in single digits. The *General Hewitt* sailed from England sometime in August 1813 with convicts from hulks at Sheerness, Portsmouth and Langston. The *Three Bees* left England in December of the same year. The *Surrey* began the voyage from England to New South Wales in February 1814. Given that death levels from disease and fever on convict ships had greatly improved by this time, the high fatality rate on these three voyages was taken seriously by the authorities. These voyages, therefore, had an impact on the future standard of convict transportation. The same could not be said of the disaster on the *Chapman*.

Was there a mutiny on the Chapman?

In his work *Mutiny: A History of Naval Insurrection* published in 1992, Leonard F. Guttridge posits a number of theories as to why mutinies happened at sea. While his work focuses on non-convict ships, there are many parallels as to why discontent can arise and some of these reasons can easily be applied to the *Chapman* voyage. Perhaps his most convincing theory is the reality that 'a ship on the ocean is a world of its own – cramped, self-contained, and prone to a unique remoteness that modern forms of communication have by no means eliminated'.[246] While many of the sailors and soldiers on the *Chapman* may have had previous nautical experience, possibly even in warfare, the voyage to Australia was still an unnatural experience. Few of them were likely to have made such a long voyage in the past and even for those that had there was no escape from the claustrophobia of the artificially created living space on the water. It is probably the case that none of the convicts below deck had ever experienced such a voyage in the past and for them there was the added emotion that this journey was almost assuredly a one-way trip with little hope of return. In many ways it appears that the ordinary sailors on a transportation ship were seen by their superiors as not much better than the convicts imprisoned below their feet. On the average vessel this created two distinct and large bodies of people, isolated at sea and existing at the mercy of more powerful forces who had access to weaponry and regarded them with disdain.

These feelings of living in isolation and possibly being held in contempt are linked to Guttridge's second potential contributor to mutiny. 'Emotions born of collective discontent,' he wrote, 'which in a larger social context may become diffused, channelled, or otherwise rendered harmless, may within the close confines of a ship, fester and turn explosive, especially during a long voyage.'[247] Many of those forced to live on the *Chapman* for four months did so in a constant state of collective discontent. It would be inconceivable to consider that 200 Irish convicts imprisoned below deck on a convict ship at the mercy of their English gaolers would not have held conversations about escaping from their perilous situation. Could it be that the convict Michael Collins *did* hear plans to overthrow the crew and take the ship to America? If so, to what extent was it likely that such conversations were borne out of a combination of bravado, boredom and animosity? Did this amount to a mutiny? Based on the oral and written testimony of the captain and surgeon-superintendent alone, it is clear that if there was an attempted mutiny from within the prison it never advanced beyond the plotting stage. The reality is that the lethal combination of 'emotions born of collective discontent', which Guttridge argued would dissolve in a less claustrophobic setting, never did come to the surface, 'fester and turn explosive' during the *Chapman* voyage in 1817.

Citing the French writer Charles Vidil, Guttridge agrees that onboard life was an ideal backdrop to 'facilitate the disturbance of the mind' while planting false rumours and enhancing the 'growth of suggestion'.[248] Again, it is important to remember that Guttridge was writing about mutiny in the context of vessels that did not contain large numbers of prisoners in the lower deck. The role of Michael Collins comes into focus once more, as the planting of rumours was essentially the catalyst to the 17 April event. Applied to the *Chapman*, under this theory the rumour is planted in the fertile ground of the disturbed minds of soldiers and officers where the possibility of a mutiny and the obvious threat is amplified by the isolation of the sea and the vulnerability of no viable means of escape. The soldiers of the *Chapman* were so flustered by a series of minor occurrences leading up to 17 April that their collective unease merely needed one more suggestion to push them over the cliff. That suggestion came from Michael Collins.

Ballyn emphasises the different responses to rumours of mutiny. On the *Chapman*, such tales 'were met with extreme brutality and sadistic behaviour' from the officers. On the *Tottenham*, they 'were met with the exact opposite: understanding, humanity and compassion'. One of the ways she accounts for the differing responses is by noting the importance of the characters of those running the ship, from the most senior to the most junior roles.[249] Given that the convict populations of both ships were not much different – with mutiny almost certainly possible on any convict ship anyway – the main factor determining the outcome is how it is handled by those with power. The humane approach of those in charge of the *Tottenham* ensured a different outcome to the brutal paranoia that led to mayhem on the *Chapman*.[250]

Despite the extensive testimony that has survived from both the convicts and wider crew of the *Chapman*, one element of their journey to which we are not privy is the private, whispered, incidental conversations that took place throughout the day and indeed the night. Guttridge notes that many of those with grievances tended to gather surreptitiously at different locations on a ship where they would discuss their problems.[251] Despite the level of monitoring and control of conversations inside the prison on this voyage, there is little doubt that the convicts had ample opportunity to hold secretive discussions at virtually any time of the night or day. Likewise, the sailors and soldiers, standing guard during many long, boring hours, as they were in the various hatchways and passages, were susceptible to suggestion and intrigue. Guttridge points out that what he terms 'all lower-deck mutinies' had one set of factors in common. This was 'a display of collective discontent never approaching the slightest semblance of a desire to overthrow authority and seize the ship'.[252] Applying this concept to the *Chapman* would suggest that while the convicts were disgruntled, perhaps about food or lack of fresh air, they were never in any real danger of attempting to take the ship. This was not what they wanted.

As this book has tried to demonstrate, the voyage of the *Chapman* from the Cove of Cork to New South Wales between March and July 1817 should have been a fairly standard operation. In a well-practised routine, many similar convict removals had taken place from England and Ireland to New South Wales by this time. Mortality rates declined to almost zero on the majority of journeys, yet the maiden transportation voyage of the *Chapman* was something of an aberration. The specific reasons for the killing, the wounding and the mayhem are many and disputed. Perhaps the most effective way to account for the misfortune that befell the voyage is to consider the coming together of a lethal combination of factors to create what became a perfect storm at sea. When suspicion, incarceration, intrigue, control, brutality, rumour, inexperience and incompetence were all brought together across oceans and seas in 1817, the inevitable conclusion was calamity.

Appendix 1

Campbell Muster Report

Copy of Muster of 176 Convicts arrived in Sydney Cove on Saturday, the 26th day of July, 1817, on board the Transport Shop Chapman, John Drake, Master, from Ireland, and taken on board said ship on Thursday, the 31st day of said July, and on Friday, the 1st day of August, By Command of His Excellency the Governor, By John Thomas Campbell, Esquire, His Excellency's Secretary. The number embarked in Ireland being 200 Men, whereof twelve were killed, and two died of Dysentery, five Wounded, and five Sick sent to the Hospital.

This consisted of a detailed statement of the convicts' names, their descriptions, complaints, etc. Among the 'complaints', 132 complained of short provisions, and others of:

Being stabbed and deprived of food event to fainting
Being wounded in heel
Losing 5 guineas by his hat being taken from him
Loss of money and clothing
Short wine, and having been shot lying in bed
Being shot in his berth, and otherwise grossly abused
Being twice wounded in bed
Being flogged and chained
Loss of clothes and money

Being starved for 11 weeks
Being beat and abused by Ship's Officer
Being stabbed by a Soldier
Having fainted from want of food; twice flogged undeserved
Mr Baxter threatened to smother prisoners with brimstone and charcoal
Mr Baxter being very cruel
Being twice flogged for speaking Irish and making a noise
Being barbarously beat by Mr Baxter with butt end of Bayonet
Being kicked and leaped upon by Mr Baxter, when chained on cable
Mr Baxter hove lemon juice in his eyes
Being chained naked with 73 others for nearly 24 hours
Having got 2 dozen for coughing, beat with cutlasses

Appendix 2 [253]

Chapman Convict Indents: Successfully Landed at Port Jackson, New South Wales

Name	Where Convicted	When	Term	Native Place	Calling	Age
James Rowe	City of Dublin	December 1814	Life	Meath	Coachman	38
James Talbot	City of Dublin	July 1815	7 years	Dublin	Sailor	28
Thomas Morris	City of Dublin	July 1815	7 years	Dublin	Sailor	28
James Morris or Murphy	City of Dublin	7 January 1815	14 years	Dublin	Farmer and Grazier	36
Thomas Higgins	City of Dublin	7 February 1816	7 years	Dublin	Labour	18
Thomas Kelly	City of Dublin	7 February 1816	7 years	Dublin	Baker	18
John Fagan	City of Dublin	7 February 1816	7 years	Dublin		

Name	Where Convicted	When	Term	Native Place	Calling	Age
Nicholas Dunne	City of Dublin	16 January 1816	14 years			22
Charles Daly				Dublin	Servant	14
David Kelly	City of Dublin	13 February 1816	7 years			
Michael Kearney or Harney						17
Patrick Holagan	City of Dublin	12 March 1816	14 years	Dublin	Dairy man	36
Michael Burne	City of Dublin	6 July 1816	7 years	Dublin		21
Thomas Sheil	City of Dublin	6 July 1816	7 years	Ringsend, Dublin	Labour	26
James Matthews	City of Dublin	25 June 1816	7 years	Westmeath	Labour	30
Denis Bryan	City of Dublin	30 April 1816	7 years	Wicklow	Labour	36
Thomas Marlow	City of Dublin	26 March 1816	7 years	Westmeath	Servant	26
James Ashe	City of Dublin	6 July 1816	14 years	Dublin	Servant	26
James Dignam	City of Dublin	16 April 1816	7 years	Dublin	Labour	19
William Dunn	City of Dublin	30 April 1816	7 years	Dublin	Shepherd and Cow Doctor	30
Edward Kelly	City of Dublin	16 April 1816	7 years	Athlone	Coachman	45
Thomas Kelly or Kenna	City of Dublin	30 April 1816	7 years	Dublin	Butcher	20
James Bryan	City of Dublin	30 April 1816	7 years	Dublin	Smith	
Thomas Connor	City of Dublin	11 June 1816	7 years	Dublin	Stone cutter	22

Name	Where Convicted	When	Term	Native Place	Calling	Age
John Brady	City of Dublin	25 June 1816	14 years	Cavan	Labour	30
William Walsh	City of Dublin	25 June 1816	7 years	Dublin	Servant	16
John Ennis	City of Dublin	6 July 1816	Life	Dublin	Apprentice to a tailor	17
Thomas Keane	City of Dublin	25 June 1816	7 years	Dublin	Labour	
Richard Jennot	City of Dublin	5 July 1816	7 years	Dublin	Tailor	20
James Flynn or Foy	City of Dublin	5 July 1816	7 years	Dublin	Labour	
William Connor	City of Dublin	25 July 1816	7 years			
John McKeon or McClune	City of Dublin	25 July 1816	14 years			
Michael Bennon or Bannon	City of Dublin	25 July 1816	7 years	Dublin	Servant	17
Morgan Kelly	City of Dublin	6 August 1816	7 years	Dublin	Carpenter	20
James Revell	City of Dublin	27 August 1816	7 years	Westmeath	Waiter	30
Robert Thomson	City of Dublin	6 August 1816	7 years	Dublin	Coach harness maker	34
Bernard McPike	City of Dublin	6 August 1816	7 years	Monaghan	Groom	20
John Matthews	City of Dublin	3 September 1816	7 years	Meath	Shop clerk	32
James or Joseph Morton	City of Dublin	10 September 1816	7 years	Dublin		16
Michael Quinn	City of Dublin	20 October 1816	14 years	Sligo	Servant	?

Name	Where Convicted	When	Term	Native Place	Calling	Age
Patrick Jennings	City of Dublin	16 April 1816	7 years	Co. Galway	Gentleman's servant	35
Michael Farrell	City of Dublin	20 May 1816	7 years	Dublin	Boatman and sailmaker	24
John Flood	City of Dublin	24 September 1816	7 years	Co. Kildare	Labourer	21
James Walsh or King	City of Dublin	24 September 1816	7 years	Co. Louth	Inn waiter	23
Michael Bennett	City of Dublin	11 October 1816	7 years	Dublin	Coach-maker and carpenter	22
George McMullin	City of Dublin	20 October 1816	7 years	Galway	Groom	22
John Flynn or O'Sullivan	City of Dublin	22 October 1816	7 years	Dublin	Blacksmith's hammerman	29
Edward Rogers	City of Dublin	22 October 1816	7 years	Monaghan	Servant	19
John Gilshenon	City of Dublin	22 October 1816	7 years	Meath	Servant	25
William Gibbon	City of Dublin	5 November 1816	7 years			
John Sloane	City of Dublin	5 November 1816	7 years	Cork city	Bricklayer	32
Edward O'Brien	City of Dublin	5 November 1816	7 years	Dublin	Labourer	27
James Mills	City of Dublin	20 January 1817	7 years	Aberdeen	Labourer	23
Thomas Jones	City of Dublin	23 July 1816	7 years			

Name	Where Convicted	When	Term	Native Place	Calling	Age
William Gibbon	City of Dublin	1816	7 years	Dublin	Baker	19
Michael Gilliffe	City of Dublin	1816	7 years	Dublin	Baker	19
George Ball	City of Dublin	1816	7 years	Dublin	Baker	19
Patrick Mooney	City of Dublin	1816	7 years	Meath	Groom	35
Michael Barrett	City of Dublin	17 December 1816	7 years	Dublin	Carter	30
James Burne	City of Dublin	17 December 1816	7 years	Wexford	Carpenter's apprentice	19
John Donally	City of Dublin	17 December 1816	7 years	Wicklow	Labourer	26
John McGinnis	City of Dublin	17 December 1816	7 years	Dublin	Servant	17
John Doyle	City of Dublin	17 December 1816	7 years	Dublin	Labourer	21
Owen Mc Daniel	City of Dublin	10 February 1816	7 years	Wexford	Servant	20
James Higgins	City of Dublin	16 September 1816	7 years	Dublin	Labourer	19
Thomas Hall	City of Dublin	25 June 1816	7 years	Dublin	Plasterer, slater and painter	32
Michael McGinnis	City of Dublin	1816	7 years	Meath	Labourer	29
Thomas Morgan	City of Dublin	7 December 1816	Life	Dublin	Fisherman and labourer	21

Name	Where Convicted	When	Term	Native Place	Calling	Age
Michael Talbot	City of Dublin	7 December 1816	Life	Dublin	Coachman and Groom	48
Michael or Mark Dungannon or	City of Dublin	January 1816	7 years	Longford	Soldier	30
John McGrath	City of Dublin	30 January 1816	7 years	Dublin	Labourer	48
John Lawlor	City of Dublin	13 February 1816	7 years	Dublin	Shoemaker	19
Patrick Murphy or Burne	City of Dublin	27 February 1816	14 years	Queen's County	Servant	32
John Ryan	City of Dublin	12 March 1816	7 years	Cork	Labourer	37
Michael Cox	City of Dublin	6 July 1816	14 years	King's County	Labourer	44
William Leo	City of Dublin	25 June 1816	7 years	Galway	Blacksmith	28
Peter Allen	City of Dublin	6 July 1816	7 years	Dublin	Servant	20
Terence Rice	City of Dublin	23 July 1816	7 years	Dublin		19
Patrick Sheridan	City of Dublin	6 August 1816	7 years	Dublin	Lawyer	20
Michael Woods or Collins	City of Dublin	6 August 1816	7 years	Dublin	Wig maker	23
William Hughes	City of Dublin	6 August 1816	7 years	Dublin	Labourer	20
David Garbally	City of Dublin	13 August 1816	7 years			
Daniel Parker	City of Dublin	28 October 1816	Life			

Name	Where Convicted	When	Term	Native Place	Calling	Age
John Fulton	City of Dublin	27 December 1816	7 years	Dublin	Shoemaker and servant	26
Patrick Smith	City of Dublin	17 February 1816	7 years	Tyrone	Gentleman's Servant	55
James Dunn	City of Dublin	5 November 1816	14 years	Gardener and nursery man	Gardener	36
Christopher Kelly	City of Dublin	16 July 1816	7 years			
William Grady	City of Dublin	16 October 1816	Life	Dublin	Tanner and horse-shoer	42
Walter Archbald	City of Dublin	16 October 1816	Life	Dublin	Labourer	20
James Trayner	County Dublin	24 October 1816	7 years	Monaghan	Servant	28
Bernard Kelly	County Dublin?	11 January 1816	14 years			
John Dooley	County Dublin?	29 April 1816	7 years	Galway	Labouring Boy	18
Thomas Kelly	County Dublin	6 July 1816	Life	Dublin	Labourer	24
Richard Caffrey	County Dublin	17 February 1816	7 years	Dublin	Labourer	22
William Ready	County Dublin	29 April 1816	14 years	Galway	Servant	26
Patrick Browne	County Dublin	16 October 1816	7 years	Dublin	Labourer	24
Thomas Mulholland	County Dublin	16 October 1816	Life			

Name	Where Convicted	When	Term	Native Place	Calling	Age
John Daly	County Dublin	16 October 1816	Life	Meath	Labourer	18
Nicholas Savage	County Dublin	16 October 1816	Life	Dublin	Shoemaker	24
John Guider	County Tipperary	Summer 1816	7 years	Tipperary	Labourer	25
Patrick Ledding	County Tipperary	Summer 1816	7 years	Co. Tipperary	Labourer	24
Philip Dwyer	County Tipperary	March 1816	7 years	Co. Tipperary	Farmer and Labourer	41
Lawrence Reilly	County Louth	Spring 1816	7 years	Dundalk	Labourer	20
Michael or Matthew McElroy	County Louth	Spring 1816	7 years	Dundalk	Labourer	23
Francis Murphy	County Louth	Summer 1816	7 years	Monaghan	Butcher	20
James Meath	County Louth	Summer 1816	7 years	Dunleer	Groom and coachman	21
James Byrne	County Louth	Summer 1816	7 years	Louth Town	Labourer	30
Philip Ward	County Louth	Summer 1816	7 years	Monaghan	Labourer	40
Patrick Finnegan	County of Louth	Summer 1816	Life	Louth	Labourer and Sailor	61
Patrick Kelly	County Dublin	Summer 1816	Life	Louth	Stable helper	22
Patrick Ward	Meath	Lent	7 years	Meath	Labourer	20
Bryan Brady	Meath	Lent	7 years	Meath	Labourer	26
James Goggin or Gaughran	Meath	Lent	7 years	Cavan	Shoemaker	23
Michael Leonard	City of Dublin	Summer 1816	14 years	Leitrim	Labourer	30
Charles Malloy	County Westmeath	March 1816	7 years	Leitrim	Labourer	29

Name	Where Convicted	When	Term	Native Place	Calling	Age
James Fox	County Westmeath	April 1816	7 years	Castle Daly Westmeath	Labourer	25
Thomas McGiff	City of Dublin	Summer 1816	Life	Westmeath	Soldier	24
Arthur Keefe	County Cork	Summer 1816	7 years	Fermoy	Servant	15
Denis Hourahan	County Cork	Summer 1816	Life	Bantry Bay	Labourer	20
Cornelius Hourahan	County Cork	Summer 1816	Life	Bantry Bay	Labourer	26
James Collins	County Cork	Summer 1816	Life			
Michael Collins	City of Dubliin	Spring 1816	7 years	Bandon	Labourer	26
John Sullivan	City of Dublin	Spring 1816	Life			
John Connor	City of Dublin	Summer 1816	Life	Bantry Bay	Labourer	80
Cornelius Connor	County Cork	Summer 1816	Life	Bantry Bay	Labourer	30
Richard Connor	County Cork	Summer 1816	Life	Bantry Bay	Labourer	20
Daniel Connor	County Cork	Summer 1816	Life	Bantry Bay	Labourer	26
Patrick Mahony	Cork City	March 1816	7 years	Leitrim	Lawyer	23
John McKenna	Monaghan	Summer 1816	7 years	Leitrim	Labourer	19
Owen Hughes	County Monaghan	Summer 1816	7 years	Leitrim	Labourer	20
John Malone	County Monaghan	Summer 1816	7 years	Leitrim		
John McDonough	County Kerry	Spring 1816	7 years	Kerry	Labourer	21
Daniel Daly	County Limerick	Spring 1816	7 years	Limerick		32
Patrick Fitzgibbon	County Limerick	Spring 1816	7 years	Limerick	Labourer	32

Name	Where Convicted	When	Term	Native Place	Calling	Age
James Roberts	City of Limerick	Spring 1816	7 years			
John Jackson	City of Limerick	Summer 1816	7 years			
Andrew McMahon	County Clare	Summer 1816	Life	Ennis	Servant	?
Andrew Kenny	County Galway	Spring 1816	7 years	Galway	Labourer	28
Matthew Daw	County Galway	Spring 1816	7 years	Roscommon	Labourer	40
Matthew Rouahan	County Galway	Spring 1816	7 years	Banagher		40
Patrick Kagan	County of Galway	Summer 1816	7 years	Galway	Labourer	40
John Kiernan or Jack Tiernan	County of Galway	Lent 1816	14 years	Leitrim	Teacher	24
John Gooley or Patrick Goaly or Devny	County of Galway	Lent 1816	7 years			
Edward Lenargan	Waterford County	Spring 1816	7 years	Waterford	Labourer	43
William Warren	Waterford City	Spring 1816	14 years	Co. Wexford	Farmer	53
Peter Pigeon	Queen's County	Summer 1816	7 years	Maryborough	Labourer	24
Edward Ging	Queen's County	Summer 1816	7 years	King's County	Butcher	29
Thomas Maher or Mahon	Queen's County	Summer 1816	7 years	Queen's County	Labourer	35
Peter Hanlan	King's County	August 1816	14 years	Tullamore	Labourer and Brick-maker	
Michael Mulpeter	King's County	August 1816	7 years	Philips Town	Labourer	

Name	Where Convicted	When	Term	Native Place	Calling	Age
John Dooley	King's County	August 1816	7 years	Maryborough	Farmer	
Cha O'Donnell	County Mayo	Summer 1816	Life	Mayo	Labourer	35
James Flynn	County Mayo	Summer 1816	7 years	Mayo	Servant	18
John Hay	County Sligo	Summer 1816	7 years	Monaghan	Herd	33
Daniel McCormack	County Sligo	Summer 1816	7 years			
James McGrady	Kilkenny City	Spring 1816	7 years	Roscommon	Servant	24
Laurence Burdon or Furlong	County Wexford	Summer 1816	7 years	Wexford	Shoemaker	21
James Martin or Mallon	County Tyrone	March 1816	7 years	Tyrone	Butcher	36
Frances Cush	County Tyrone	March 1816	Life	Tyrone	Weaver and Pedlar	37
James Gubbey	County Tyrone	March 1816	7 years	Dungannon	Servant	21
Edward Donahoe	County Tyrone	August 1816	7 years	Limerick City	Seaman	24
Patrick Hunt	County Kildare	March 1816	7 years	Naas	Butcher	25
Andrew Minla or Murtagh	County Kildare	April 1816	7 years	Meath	Labourer	30
James Hayes	County Kildare	July 1816	7 years	Athy	Labourer	21
Edward Jameson	County of Down	March 1815?	7 years	Downpatrick	Labourer	39
Cha Malone	County of Down	August 1815?	7 years	Tyrone	Riddlemaker	51
John Lindon	County of Down	March 1816	7 years	Co. Down	Weaver	20

Name	Where Convicted	When	Term	Native Place	Calling	Age
William Murray	County of Down	March 1816	7 years	Co. Down	Labourer	24
Terence Kiernan	Drogheda	July 1816	7 years	Cooks Town, Co. Tyrone	Training for a priest	27
Hugh McPike	Londonderry	March 1816	7 years	Co. Down	Weaver	37
Owen Dignum	County Longford	July 1816	14 years	Leitrim	Labourer	36
Oliver Wallace	County Longford	March 1816	Life			
Charles Connell	County Longford	March 1816	Life	Longford	Labourer	40
Owen Tunny	County of Roscommon	Summer 1816	7 years	Co. Sligo	Labourer	28
James Tonson or Johnson	County of Roscommon	Summer 1816	7 years	Roscommon	Labourer	40
John Dempsey	County Roscommon	August 1815	7 years	Longford	Seaman	28
John Murray	County Antrim	March 1816	14 years	Longford	Clerk	38
Robert Belfour	County Antrim	March 1816	14 years	Belfast	Tailor and Labourer	16
Loughlin McCleare	County Antrim	March 1816	14 years			
Bernard Woods	County Antrim	March 1816	14 years	Monaghan	Weaver	15
John Blakely	County Antrim	Summer 1816	14 years			
Patrick McKenna	County Antrim	Summer 1816	Life	Co. Meath	Groom and Coachman	25
Robert Nesbitt	County Antrim	Summer 1816	7 years			
Philip McBride	County Antrim	Summer 1816	7 years	Belfast	Labourer	18
Michael McNally	County Antrim	Summer 1816	Life	Co. Derry	Labourer	33

Name	Where Convicted	When	Term	Native Place	Calling	Age
John Young	County Antrim	Summer 1816	7 years	Antrim	Labourer	31
George Stephenson	County Antrim	Summer 1816	7 years			
William Hare	County Antrim	Summer 1816	7 years	Co. Down	Labourer	18
Dominick Mc__?	County Antrim	Summer 1816	Life	Tyrone	Labourer	40
Hugh Gordon	County Armagh	Spring 1816	Life	Armagh	Shoemaker	26
Patrick McCusker	County Armagh	Spring 1816	Life	Armagh	Liner weaver	40
George Campbell	County Armagh	Spring 1816	7 years	Armagh	Cotton weaver	34
John McArdell	County Armagh	Summer 1816	14 years			
John Quinn	County Armagh	Summer 1816	7 years	Armagh	Labourer	20
Christopher Quinn	County Wicklow	March 1816	7 years			
John Doyle	County Wicklow	March 1816	7 years	Wicklow	Weaver	26
Loughlin Bryan	County Wicklow	Summer 1816	Life	Wicklow	Shepherd	30

Appendix 3

Chapman Roll of the Dead

Convicts

Lauchlan McLean

Tried and convicted for robbery in Belfast in 1816, Lauchlan McLean or Laughlin McCleare, as his name sometimes appeared in official records, was sentenced to fourteen years' transportation. McClean was the first convict to lose his life as a result of gunfire on the *Chapman*. He was one of three men to lose his life during the night of the first shooting. His body was cast into the sea somewhere to the west of Africa on the afternoon of 18 April 1817.

Daniel McCormick

McCormick died during the first shooting on the night of 17 April and his body was buried at sea the following day. At twenty-eight years old, the Sligo native was convicted of robbery and sentenced to transportation for seven years.

George Stephenson

He boarded the *Chapman* at the age of thirty-five, having been convicted in the summer of 1816 of stealing money in Belfast. He was sentenced to seven years' transportation but he lost his life during the gunfire on the night of 17 April.

Thomas Mullholland

Mulholland was believed to have lived a daring life as a highway robber on the roads leading in and out of Dublin. His criminal career ended following his arrest at a public house in Cook Street in the city in September 1816. Some nights earlier he and other members of his gang overpowered and robbed a blacksmith on the road at Donnybrook. A sentence of death was commuted to transportation. Mulholland lost his life on 21 April 1817 as a result of the shooting on the *Chapman* four days earlier.

James Roberts

At a court in Limerick in January 1816, James Roberts and an accomplice named Mary Godfrey were convicted of 'coining' tokens of the Bank of Ireland. A number of implements used for coining were found in their possession. Roberts was sentenced to seven years' transportation. In December of 1816 an order was granted to remove him from Limerick prison (where he had been waiting all year) and transfer him to Cork, where he would await transportation on the *Chapman*. On 23 April 1817 he became the fifth convict to die as a result of the first shooting episode at sea.

Daniel Parker

A thirty-six-year-old horse thief from Dublin, Parker was convicted at Dublin City Sessions in 1815. His death sentence was commuted to one of transportation but on 25 April he succumbed to the wounds he sustained during the shooting of the previous week.

John McArdell

The thirty-year-old Armagh convict was the first convict to die during the second shooting event. McArdell was convicted of stealing forged notes and sentenced to fourteen years' transportation the previous year. His killing became the subject of a murder trial at the Admiralty Sessions in London less than two years later.

Bryan Kelly

In January 1816 the twenty-eight-year-old was convicted in a Dublin courtroom of being in possession of forged notes. He is believed to have been the second convict to die as a result of the 28 April shooting incident. He did not lose his life in the prison but on the poop deck, where he was confined with a number of other prisoners. Intelligence provided to the officers by Bryan Kelly is alleged to have contributed to the cause of that night's events.

Oliver Wallace
Wallace was the only convict on the *Chapman* to be convicted of murder. His sentence was transportation for life, almost certainly commuted from execution. The thirty-five-year-old died the day after the second shooting, but he was not caught up in that incident, instead succumbing to wounds sustained during the event of 17 April. His was clearly a prolonged death, coming as it did some eleven days after he was shot.

John Jackson
Jackson was one of those detained in the jolly boat on the night of 24 May when it was fired upon by the military guard. The twenty-six-year-old was convicted of robbery in Limerick the previous year. He did not die immediately from his wounds but suffered a number of days before passing away.

John Malone
On 26 May, thirty-one-year-old John Malone from Monaghan became the latest victim to die of gunshot wounds. It is unclear in which of the shooting incidents Malone received his injuries but the housebreaker, whose sentence was also commuted from execution to transportation, had clearly suffered an agonising and lengthy journey to his death.

James Collins
Towards the end of May 1817, fifty-seven-year-old James Collins from Cork passed away from an unspecified cause. Collins was another unfortunate convict who had escaped the hangman's noose in favour of permanent exile to New South Wales.

Christopher Kelly
His is the last known convict death on this voyage of the *Chapman*. The forty-one-year-old vagrant from Dublin died from an unspecified cause.

His offence, the reason for his expulsion to New South Wales, was that of vagrancy.

Members of the Extended Crew

George Murray
George Murray was a sailor and likely one of the first to lose his life on the voyage. Soon after the shooting commenced on 17 April he was caught in the crossfire and shot in the torso. He died instantly.

William Kendrick
Nothing is recorded about the death of William Kendrick. His death on 22 May 1817 was noted in the official journal of Captain Drake with no indication that is was connected to any of the violent occurrences that took place on the ship.

Francis Lucy
The sailor Francis Lucy, sometimes incorrectly recorded as Francis Lucas, was killed on 24 May by one of the soldiers. Lucy was chained in the jolly boat with two other sailors and the convict John Jackson. After being wounded in an initial firing he was subsequently shot point blank in the head by a soldier named Hogan.

Appendix 4

New South Wales, Australia, Certificates of Freedom, 1810–1814, 1827–1867[254]

Number	Certificate Date	Name	Native Place	Occupation	Sentence
27/879	12 September 1827	Robert Belfour	Belfast	Tailor and Labourer	7 years
196/2786	29 September 1824	Laurence Bourdon	Wexford	Shoemaker	7 years
56/1695	18 December 1823	James Burne	Wexford	Carpenter	7 years
16/4368	6 October 1825	Thomas Connor	Dublin	Stone Mason	7 years
28/12	7 January 1828	John Dempsey	Roscommon	Labourer	Additional year
30/594	21 August 1830	Owen Dignum	Antrim	Labourer	14 years
30/673	5 November 1830	James Dunn	Queen's County	Gardener	14 years
92/5994		James Flynn	Mayo	Labourer	7 years
31/2306	5 July 1824	David Garbally	Dublin	Labourer	7 years

Number	Certificate Date	Name	Native Place	Occupation	Sentence
34/1390	17 October 1834	Peter Hanlan	King's County	Labourer	14 years
30/230	26 April 1830	Patrick Jennings	Galway	Labourer	14 years
27/899	15 September 1827	James Johnson	Roscommon	Labourer	7 years
27/2852	14 October 1824	Thomas Keane	Dublin	Labourer	7 years
45/4677	19 September 1825	Arthur Keefe	Cork	Labourer	7 years
30/733	1 November 1830	John or James Kiernan	Leitrim	Teacher and Stone Mason	14 years
34/1141	18 September 1834	Michael Leonard	Leitrim	Labourer	14 years
37/362	26 April 1837	James Martin	Tyrone	Butcher	7 years
57/1696	18 December 1823	John McGinnis	Dublin	Labourer	7 years
33/400	25 April 1833	Philip McBride	Belfast	Labourer	7 years
35/862	10 August 1835	James McGrady	Roscommon	Servant	7 years
28/265	10 April 1828	John McKenna	Monaghan	Labourer	7 years
32/675	25 July 1832	John McKeon	Dublin		14 years
60/1189	9 March 1826	James Meath	Louth	Labourer	7 years
14/17/11	10 January 1824	James Mills	Aberdeen	Labourer	7 years
28/778	20 August 1828	Andrew Minte	Westmeath	Labourer	7 years
4/1643	4 December 1823	Patrick Mooney	Meath	Gardener and Coachman	7 years

Number	Certificate Date	Name	Native Place	Occupation	Sentence
43/315	27 February 1843	Peter Pidgeon	Maryborough	Labourer	7 years
207/2797	20 September 1824	Christopher Quinn	Wicklow	Labourer	7 years
10/1703	2 January 1824	Edward Rogers	Monaghan	Carpenter and country servant	7 years
54/1751	20 January 1824	Pat Sheerdan	Dublin	Lawyer	7 years
40/143	26 March 1830	William Warren	Wexford	Labourer	14 years
30/145	26 March 1830	Nicholas Dunne	King's County	Labourer	14 years
27/915	22 September 1827	Bernard Wood	Antrim	Linen weaver and lawyer	7 years
223/2813	30 September 1824	John Young	Antrim	Weaver	7 years

Appendix 5

Chapman Convicts Pardoned

Name	Birth Year	Arrival	Year	Pardon
Patrick Fagan	1799	1817	1849	Conditional
Hugh Gordon		1817	1821	Absolute
Cornelius Hourahan	1802	1817	1843	Conditional
John Kiernan		1817	1821	Absolute
Andrew McMahon		1817	1848	Conditional
Michael McElroy		1817	1821	Absolute
Dominick McIllhatton		1817	1835	

Appendix 6

Chapman Ticket of Leave Convicts

Name	Birth Year	Date of Ticket
Laughlin Bryan	1787	14 August 1829
Loughlin Bryan	1787	26 July 1831
Loughlin Bryan	1787	11 May 1836
Cornelius Connor	1784	26 April 1837
James Dunn	1784	31 March 1827
Patrick Fagan	1799	5 August 1827
Patrick Fagan	1799	6 April 1836
Patrick Fagan	1799	3 February 1838
Patrick Fagan	1799	8 February 1838
Cornelius Hourahan		26 April 1837
Cornelius Hourahan		18 April 1839
Cornelius Hourahan		1 February 1840
Cornelius Hourahan		28 August 1840
Cornelius Hourahan		29 October 1841
Cornelius Hourahan		6 October 1842
Michael Leonard	1786	26 August 1824
Michael Leonard	1786	6 October 1825
Domh McIlhatton	1777	11 August 1825
Domh McIlhatton	1777	20 July 1833

Name	Birth Year	Date of Ticket
Andrew McMahon		30 December 1843
Michael McNally	1786	2 February 1826
Michael McNally	1786	31 July 1826
Michael Talbot	1772	3 December 1832
William Warren	1770	15 December 1825
William Warren	1770	20 October 1828

Appendix 7

Convict Voyages from Ireland to New South Wales 1791–1849

Extracted from *The Convict Ships, 1787–1868*, by Charles Bateson. 2nd ed. 1974 and http://members.iinet.net.au/~perthdps/convicts/shipNSW2.html

Accurate death rates not available post-1800.

Vessel	Departure	Year	Male	Female	Deaths
Queen	Cork	1791	133	22	7
Boddingtons	Cork	1793	125	20	1
Sugar Cane	Cork	1793	110	50	1
Marquis Cornwallis	Cork	1795	163	70	11
Britannia	Cork	1796	144	44	11
Minerva	Cork	1799	165	26	3
Friendship	Cork	1799	133		19
Anne I	Cork	1800	147	24	
Hercules I	Ireland	1801	140	25	
Atlas I	Ireland	1801	151	28	
Atlas II	Cork	1802	208		
Rolla	Cork	1802	127	37	
Tellicherry	Cork	1805	130	36	
William Pitt	Cork	1805	1	120	

Vessel	Departure	Year	Male	Female	Deaths
Experiment II	Cork	1809		60	
Boyd	Cork	1809	139		
Archduke Charles	Cork	1812	147	54	
Canada	Cork	1814	160		
Francis and Eliza	Cork	1814	54	69	
Alexander II	Ireland	1815		84	
Guilford	Ireland	1815	228		
Surry I	Cork	1816	150		
Chapman	Cork	1817	200		13
Pilot	Cork	1817	119		
Canada	Cork	1817		89	
Guilford	Cork	1817	204		
Minerva I	Ireland	1818	160		
Elizabeth I	Cork	1818		101	
Earl St Vincent	Cork	1818	160		
Tyne	Ireland		180		
Bencoolen	Cork	1819	150		
Mary I	Cork	1819	160		
Daphne	Cork	1819	180		
Minerva I	Cork	1819	172		
Lord Wellington	Cork			121	
Castle Forbes	Cork	1819	140		
Janus	Cork	1819		105	
Hadlow	Cork	1820	150		
Dorothy	Cork	1820	190		
Prince Regent II	Cork	1820	144		
Lord Sidmouth	Cork	1820	175		
John Barry	Cork	1821	180		
John Bull	Cork	1821		80	
Southworth	Cork	1821	101		
Isabella I	Cork	1821	200		
Mangles	Cork	1822	191		
Countess of Harcourt	Cork	1822	172		
Brampton	Cork	1822	172		
Woodman	Cork	1823		97	

Vessel	Departure	Year	Male	Female	Deaths
Recovery	Cork	1823	180		
Earl St Vincent	Cork	1823	157		
Isabella I	Ireland		201		
Medina	Cork	1823	180		
Castle Forbes	Cork	1823	140		
Prince Regent I	Cork	1824	180		
Almorah	Cork	1824		109	
Ann and Amelia	Cork	1824	200		
Asia I	Cork	1824	190		
Hooghly	Cork	1825	195		
Mariner	Cork	1825		113	
Lonach	Cork	1825	144		
Henry Porcher	Dublin	1825	176		
Sir Godfrey Webster	Cork	1825	196		
Mangles	Cork	1825	190		
Lady Rowena	Cork	1826		100	
Regalia	Dublin	1826	130		
Boyne	Cork	1826	200		
Phoenix III	Dublin	1826	190		
Brothers	Cork	1826		161	
Mariner	Cork	1827	161		
Countess of Harcourt	Dublin	1827	194		
Cambridge	Dublin	1827	200		
Eliza II	Cork	1827	192		
Elizabeth II	Cork	1827		194	
Marquis of Huntley	Cork	1827	160		
Morley	Dublin	1827	195		
Mangles	Dublin	1828	200		
Borodino	Cork	1828	200		
City of Edinburgh	Cork	1828		80	
Governor Ready	Cork	1828	200		
Sophia	Dublin	1828	192		
Fergusson	Dublin	1828	216		
Edward	Cork	1829		177	
Eliza II	Cork	1829	171		

Vessel	Departure	Year	Male	Female	Deaths
Guilford	Dublin	1829	200		
Larkins	Cork	1829	200		
Asia I	Cork	1829		200	
James Pattison	Dublin	1829	200		
Forth I	Cork	1830	118		
Forth II	Cork	1830		120	
Hercules II	Dublin	1830	200		
Florentia	Ireland	1830	200		
Andromeda II	Cork	1830	181		
Edward	Cork	1830	158		
Waterloo	Dublin	1830	200		
Palambam	Cork	1831		116	
Hooghly	Cork	1831		186	
Jane I	Cork	1831	130		
Asia V	Cork	1831	220		
Bussorah Merchant	Dublin	1831	200		
Norfolk	Cork	1831	200		
Pyramus	Cork	1831		151	
Captain Cook	Dublin	1831	200		
Southwood	Cork	1832		134	
City of Edinburgh	Cork	1832	145		
Eliza II	Cork	1832	198		
Dunvegan Castle	Dublin	1832	200		
Roslin Castle	Cork	1832	199		
Surrey II	Cork	1832		142	
Portland	Cork	1833	193		
Caroline	Cork	1833		120	
Royal Admiral	Dublin	1833	221		
Java	Cork	1833	206		
Royal Sovereign	Dublin	1833	170		
Parmelia	Cork	1833	220		
James Laing	Dublin	1834	201		
Andromeda II	Cork	1834		176	
Blenheim I	Cork	1834	200		
Royal Admiral	Dublin	1834	208		

Vessel	Departure	Year	Male	Female	Deaths
Forth	Cork	1834	196		
Hero	Dublin	1835	202		
Lady Macnaghten	Dublin	1835	305		
Neva (wrecked)	Cork	1835		151	
Hive (wrecked)	Ireland	1835	252		
Roslin Castle	Cork	1835		165	
Surrey I	Cork	1836	229		
Thomas Harrison	Cork	1836		112	
Waterloo	Cork	1836	224		
Captain Cook	Cork	1836	236		
Pyramus	Cork	1836		121	
Earl Grey	Cork	1836	297		
St Vincent	Cork	1836	193		
Margaret	Cork	1837		162	
Heber	Dublin	1837	243		
Calcutta II	Dublin	1837	360		
Sir Charles Forbes	Dublin	1837		150	
Neptune II	Dublin	1837	200		
Diamond	Cork	1837		162	
William Jardine	Dublin	1837	224		
Westmoreland	Dublin	1838	254		
Clyde I	Dublin	1838	216		
Elphinstone	Dublin	1838	255		
Margaret	Dublin	1838		189	
Waverley	Dublin	1839	176		
Whitby	Dublin	1839		133	
Blenheim I	Dublin	1839	207		
Minerva II	Dublin	1839		119	
Middlesex	Dublin	1839	200		
Nautilus	Dublin	1839	200		
Isabella II	Dublin	1840		119	
King William	Dublin	1840	180		
Margaret	Dublin	1840		133	
Pekoe	Dublin	1840	184		
Havering	Dublin	1849	336		

Notes

Introduction

1 Clive Emsley, *Crime, police, and penal policy: European experiences 1750–1940* (Oxford University Press: Oxford, 2007), p. 35.

2 Helen Johnston, *Crime in England 1815–1880: experiencing the criminal justice system* (London, 2015), p. 73.

3 Joan Kavanagh and Dianne Snowden, *Van Diemen's women: a history of transportation to Tasmania* (The History Press Ireland: Dublin, 2015), p. 25.

4 John Hirst, 'The Australian experience: the convict colony' in Norval Morris and David J. Rothman (eds) *The Oxford History of the Prison: the practice of punishment in western society* (Oxford University Press: Oxford, 1998), p. 238.

5 Con Costello, 'The convicts: transportation from Ireland' in Colm Kiernan (ed.) *Australia and Ireland 1788–1988: bicentenary essays* (Gill and Macmillan: Dublin, 1986), p. 119.

6 Malcolm Campbell, *Ireland's new worlds: immigrants, politics and society in the United States and Australia, 1815–1922* (Wisconsin, 2008), p. 12.

7 Seán O'Toole, *The History of Australian corrections* (University of New South Wales Press, 2006), p. 22.

8 Kenneth Morgan, *The birth of industrial Britain: social change, 1750–1850* (Pearson: London, 2004), p. 96.

9   Rena Lohan, 'Sources in the National Archives for research into the transportation of Irish convicts to Australia 1791–1853 (www.nationalarchives.ie/topics/transportation/transp1.html) (11 July 2016).

10 Report of the commissioners appointed by the Crown to investigate certain alleged abuses in the Convict Department at Cork; together with the evidence taken before them, 1817, p. 1.

11 See Tim Carey, *Mountjoy: the story of a prison* (The Collins Press: Cork, 2000).

12 *Report from the Select Committee on Transportation*, 10 July 1812, p. 3.

13 *Report from the Select Committee on Transportation*, 10 July 1812, p. 3.

14 Robert Adams, *Prison riots in Britain and the USA* (Macmillan, 1994), p. 109.

15 John Black, *An authentic narrative of the mutiny on board the ship Lady Shore; with particulars of a journey through part of Brazil* (London, 1798), pp. 3–4.

16 Robert Hughes, *The Fatal Shore* (London, 2003), p. 156.

17 Hamish Maxwell-Stewart, 'Those lads contrived a plan: attempts at mutiny on Australia-bound convict vessels', in *International Review of Social History* (September 2013), 192.

18 Maxwell-Stewart, 'Those lads contrived a plan', p. 179.

19 Robert Adams, *Prison riots in Britain and the USA* (Macmillan, 1994), p. 109–10.

20 http://searcharchives.bl.uk/primo_library/libweb/action/dlDisplay.do?docId=IAMS045-001114738&fn=permalink&vid=IAMS_VU2

21 https://convictrecords.com.au/ships/chapman

1 The Countdown to Chaos

22 *Freeman's Journal*, 12 June 1816.

23 *Freeman's Journal*, 10 July 1816.

24 George Tyner, *The traveller's guide through Ireland being an accurate and complete companion to Captain Alexander Taylor's Map of Ireland* (Byrne: Dublin, 1794), p. 71.

25 Henry D. Inglis, *Ireland in 1834: A journey throughout Ireland during the spring, summer, and autumn of 1834* (Whittaker and Co.: London, 1834), pp. 192–4.

26 Inglis, *Ireland in 1834*, p. 194.

27 Janet MacDonald, *The British Navy's Victualling Board, 1793–1815: management competence and incompetence* (The Boydell Press: Woodbridge, 2010), p. 16.

28 Report of the commissioners, 1817, p. 10.

29 Foxhall, *Health, medicine, and the sea*, p. 21.

30 Report of the commissioners, 1817, p. 18.

31 Report of the commissioners, 1817, p. 18.

32 Historical Records of Australia (HRA), *Captain's Journal*, vol. 1, no. ix, 563.

33 HRA, *Report of Judge-Advocate Wylde and Wentworth*, vol. 1, no. ix, 613.

34 HRA, *Transport Commissioners to Captain Drake*, 3 December 1816, vol. 1, no. ix, 603–4.

35 HRA, *Transport Commissioners to Captain Drake*, 3 December 1816, vol. 1, no. ix, 603–4.

36 Kevin Brown, *Poxed and scurvied: the story of sickness and health at sea* (London, 2010), pp. 121–2.

37 Kim Humphrey, 'A new era of existence: convict transportation and the authority of the surgeon in colonial Australia', *Labour History*, 59 (November, 1990), 63.

38 John McDonald and Ralph Shlomowitz, 'Mortality on convict voyages to Australia, 1788–1868', *Social Science History*, 13, 3 (Autumn, 1989), 289.

39 HRA, *Transport Commissioners to Dewar*, 28 November, vol. 1, no. ix, 601–3.

40 HRA, *Transport Commissioners to Dewar*, 28 November, vol. 1, no. ix, 601–3.

41 HRA, *Transport Commissioners to Dewar*, 28 November, vol. 1, no. ix, 601–3.

42 HRA, *Transport Commissioners to Dewar*, 28 November, vol. 1, no. ix, 601–3.

43 Robert Hughes, *The Fatal Shore* (London, 2003), p. 150.

44　HR, *Report of Judge-Advocate Wylde and Wentworth,* vol. 1, no. ix, p. 613.

45　HRA, *Dewar evidence to Wentworth Committee,* vol. 1, no. ix, p. 592–3.

46　*Chapman,* passenger list.

47　*Chapman,* transportation register, 1817.

48　New South Wales and Tasmania, Australia Convict Musters, 1806–1849, www.ancestry.com (accessed on 28 April 2016).

49　*Freeman's Journal,* 10 December 1816.

50　*Freeman's Journal,* 12 September 1816.

51　*Chapman,* transportation register, 1817.

52　*Chapman,* transportation register, 1817.

53　*Freeman's Journal,* 28 February 1816.

54　*Chapman,* transportation register, 1817.

55　The word 'prosecutor' here is not a legal one but rather a term used in newspaper reporting to describe an accuser.

56　*Freeman's Journal,* 15 June 1816.

57　*Freeman's Journal,* 28 June 1816.

2 Bloodshed in a Tropical Climate

58　Report of the commissioners, 1817, p. 1.

59　*Chapman,* transportation register, 1817.

60　*Chapman,* transportation register, 1817.

61　HRA, *Captain's Journal,* vol. 1, no. ix, p. 564.

62　Thomas Reid, *Two voyages to New South Wales and Van Diemen's Land with a description of the present condition of that interesting colony* (Longman, London: 1822), p. 13.

63　Reid, *Two voyages to New South Wales and Van Diemen's Land,* p. 15.

64　Susan Ballyn, 'Brutality versus common sense: the 'mutiny ships', the *Tottenham* and the *Chapman*', in Anna Haebich and Baden Offord (eds), *Landscapes of exile: once perilous, now safe* (Oxford, 2006), p. 36.

65　HRA, *Report of Judge-Advocate Wylde and Wentworth,* vol. 1, no. ix, p. 614.

66　HRA, *Report of Judge-Advocate Wylde and Wentworth,* vol. 1, no. ix, p. 615.

67 *Morning Post*, 6 September 1817.

68 *Truth*, 1954.

69 *Dublin Evening Post*, 20 August 1816.

70 *Belfast Newsletter*, 2 August 1816.

71 *Freemans Journal*, 26 September 1815.

72 Captain John Drake's brother Richard, was also a lower-ranking member of the officer class on the voyage.

73 *Truth*, 1954.

74 *Exeter Flying Post*, 21 January 1819.

75 *Truth*, 1954.

3 Escalation

76 HRA, *Report of Judge-Advocate Wylde and Wentworth,* vol. 1, no. ix, p. 627.

77 *Belfast Newsletter*, 2 August 1816.

78 *Freemans Journal*, 24 July 1816.

79 HRA, *Report of Judge-Advocate Wylde and Wentworth,* vol. 1, no. ix, p. 630.

80 HRA, *Report of Judge-Advocate Wylde and Wentworth,* vol. 1, no. ix, p. 630–1.

81 Foxhall, *Health, medicine and the sea*, p. 99.

82 Christine Quigley, *The corpse: a history* (McFarland & Company: Jefferson, 1996), p. 95–6.

83 HRA, *Statement of William Leo,* vol. 1, no. ix, p. 583–4.

84 *Freeman's Journal*, 13 September 1816.

85 *Freeman's Journal*, 26 July 1816.

86 *Freeman's Journal*, 11 June 1816.

87 *Freeman's Journal*, 29 August 1816.

4 Shockwaves at Sea

88 *Truth*, 7 November 1954.

89 Sean O'Toole, *The history of Australian corrections* (University of New South Wales Press, Sydney: 2006), p. 27.

90   HRA, *Statement of Surgeon Superintendent Dewar,* vol. 1, no. ix, p. 594–5.

91   HRA, *Statement of Surgeon Superintendent Dewar,* vol. 1, no. ix, p. 594–5.

92   HRA, *Report of Judge-Advocate Wylde and Wentworth,* vol. 1, no. ix, p. 615.

93   O'Toole, *A history of Australian corrections,* p. 26.

94   Hamish Maxwell-Stewart, 'The rise and fall of penal transportation' in Paul Knepper and Anja Johansen (eds) *The Oxford Handbook of Crime and Criminal Justice* (Oxford University Press, Oxford: 2016), p. 646.

95   HRA, *Medical Surgical Journal and Diary of the Convict Ship Chapman,* vol. 1, no. ix, p. 571.

96   Dungannon's name does not appear in the convict passenger list or muster roll for the *Chapman* so he may have been a sailor serving a punishment.

97   *Freeman's Journal,* 19 March 1816.

98   Kenna is also not listed in the convict passenger list or muster roll.

99   HRA, *Captain Drake's Journal,* vol. 1, no. ix, p. 563–70.

100 It is likely that not every flogging incident was written down as there are gaps in the records.

101 HRA, *Captain Drake's Journal,* vol. 1, no. ix, p. 563–70.

102 HRA, *Captain Drake's Journal,* vol. 1, no. ix, p. 563–70.

103 HRA, *Statement of Nelson,* vol. 1, no. ix, p. 770.

104 HRA, *Statement of Jones,* vol. 1, no. ix, p. 772.

105 HRA, *Statement of Jennings,* vol. 1, no. ix, p. 771.

106 HRA, *Dewar to Drake,* vol. 1, no. ix, p. 608.

107 HRA, *Drake to Dewar,* vol. 1, no. ix, p. 563–70. p. 607.

108 HRA, *Statement of Captain Drake,* vol. 1, no. ix, p. 586–91.

109 HRA, *Report of Judge-Advocate Wylde and Wentworth,* vol. 1, no. ix, p. 641.

110 HRA, *Report of Secretary J. T. Campbell,* vol. 1, no. ix, p. 645–9.

111 A general return of sick killed and wounded on board the convict ship *Chapman* between the 14th day of March and the 26th July, 1817.

5 *Aftershocks*

112 Grace Karskens, 'The dialogue of townscape: the rocks and Sydney, 1788–1820', *Australian Historical Studies*, 27, 108 (1997), p. 88.

113 *Sydney Gazette and New South Wales Advertiser*, 26 July 1817.

114 O'Toole, *A history of Australian corrections*, p. 28.

115 Dewar Journal.

116 HRA, *General order re muster of convicts on ship Chapman*, 28 July 1817, vol. 1, no. ix, p. 608.

117 Australian Dictionary of Biography, John Thomas Campbell, http://adb.anu.edu.au/biography/campbell-john-thomas-1873 accessed 31 August 2017; Keith Robert Binney, *Horsemen of the first frontier 1788–1900 and the serpent's legacy* (Volcanic: Sydney), p. 67.

118 *Truth*, 7 November 1954.

119 HRA, *Secretary Campbell to Governor Macquarie*, 1 August 1817, vol. 1, no. ix, p. 652.

120 HRA, *Secretary Campbell to Governor Macquarie*, 1 August 1817, vol. 1, no. ix, p. 652.

121 HRA, *Secretary Campbell to Governor Macquarie*, 1 August 1817, vol. 1, no. ix, p. 652.

122 HRA, *Secretary Campbell to Governor Macquarie*, 1 August 1817, vol. 1, no. ix, p. 652.

123 HRA, *Secretary Campbell to Governor Macquarie*, 1 August 1817, vol. 1, no. ix, p. 652.

124 HRA, *Secretary Campbell to Governor Macquarie*, 1 August 1817, vol. 1, no. ix, p. 652.

125 HRA, *Secretary Campbell to Governor Macquarie*, 1 August 1817, vol. 1, no. ix, p. 652.

126 HRA, *Secretary Campbell to Governor Macquarie*, 1 August 1817, vol. 1, no. ix, p. 652.

127 See Appendix – Campbell Muster Report

128 HRA, *Secretary Campbell to Governor Drake*, 1 August 1817, vol. 1, no. ix, p. 655.

129 This report is transcribed in Appendix one.

130 HRA, *Report on survey of prison on ship Chapman*, 4 August 1817, vol. 1, no. ix, p. 656.

131 HRA, *Campbell to Piper*, 9 August 1817, vol. 1, no. ix, p. 656.

132 HRA, *Warrant appointing Committee of Inquiry*, 13 August 1817, vol. 1, no. ix, p. 657–8.

133 HRA, *Thomas Wylde to Drake*, 15 August 1817, vol. 1, no. ix, p. 609.

134 HRA, *Drake to Campbell*, 19 August 1817, vol. 1, no. ix, p. 659.

135 HRA, *Campbell to Wentworth*, 19 August 1817, vol. 1, no. ix, p. 660.

136 Australian Dictionary of Biography, *Sir John Wylde* http://adb.anu.edu.au/biography/wylde-sir-john-2822 (accessed 5 September 2017)

137 Australian Dictionary of Biography, *D'Arcy Wentworth* http://adb.anu.edu.au/biography/wentworth-darcy-1545 (accessed 5 September 2017)

138 It has not been determined whether Baxter testified at this stage or alternatively, if he did appear before the inquiry but the testimony did not survive.

139 HRA, *Drake to Thomas Wylde*, 20 August 1817, vol. 1, no. ix, p. 609.

140 HRA, *Drake to Macquarie*, 4 September 1817, vol. 1, no. ix, p. 661.

141 HRA, *Campbell to Drake*, 8 September 1817, vol. 1, no. ix, p. 661.

142 HRA, *Drake to Macquarie*, 14 October 1817, vol. 1, no. ix, p. 663–4.

143 HRA, *Drake to Macquarie*, 28 October 1817, vol. 1, no. ix, p. 665.

144 HRA, *Drake to Macquarie*, 29 October 1817, vol. 1, no. ix, p. 665.

145 HRA, *Drake to Macquarie*, 3 November 1817, vol. 1, no. ix, p. 665–6.

146 HRA, *Wylde to Macquarie*, 9 November 1817, vol. 1, no. ix, p. 667–8.

147 HRA, *Wylde to Macquarie*, 9 November 1817, vol. 1, no. ix, p. 667–8.

148 HRA, *Wylde-Wentworth Report*, 15 November 1817, vol. 1, no. ix, p. 642.

149 HRA, *Wylde-Wentworth Report*, 15 November 1817, vol. 1, no. ix, p. 642.

150 HRA, *Wylde-Wentworth Report*, 15 November 1817, vol. 1, no. ix, p. 643.

151 HRA, *Wylde-Wentworth Report*, 15 November 1817, vol. 1, no. ix, p. 643.

152 HRA, *Wylde-Wentworth Report*, 15 November 1817, vol. 1, no. ix, p. 644–5.

153 HRA, *Campbell Report*, 15 November 1817, vol. 1, no. ix, p. 646.

154 HRA, *Campbell Report*, 15 November 1817, vol. 1, no. ix, p. 646–7.

155 HRA, *Campbell Report*, 15 November 1817, vol. 1, no. ix, p. 647.

156 HRA, *Campbell Report*, 15 November 1817, vol. 1, no. ix, p. 644.

6 Judgement

157 HRA, *Campbell Report*, 15 November 1817, vol. 1, no. ix, p. 648.

158 HRA, *Campbell Report*, 15 November 1817, vol. 1, no. ix, p. 648–9.

159 *Truth*, 7 November 1954.

160 Stuart Macintyre, *A concise history of Australia* (Cambridge, 2006), p. 46–7.

161 Brian Fletcher, 'Lachlan Macquarie' in David Clune and Ken Turner (eds), *The governors of New South Wales 1788–2010* (The Federation Press: Sydney, 2009), p. 115.

162 HRA, *Macquarie to Wylde*, 17 November 1817, vol. 1, no. ix, p. 669.

163 C.H. Currey, 'Baronn Field' in *Australian Dictionary of Biography* http://adb.anu.edu.au/biography/field-barron-2041 (accessed 12 September 2017).

164 HRA, *Macquarie to Wylde*, 17 November 1817, vol. 1, no. ix, p. 669.

165 HRA, *Wylde to Field*, 17 November 1817, vol. 1, no. ix, p. 670.

166 HRA, *Field to Wylde*, 18 September 1817, vol. 1, no. ix, pp. 695–6.

167 HRA, *Field to Wylde*, 29 September 1817, vol. 1, no. ix, pp. 697.

168 HRA, *Macquarie to Wylde*, 18 November 1817, vol. 1, no. ix, p. 672.

169 HRA, *Wylde to Macquarie*, 17 November 1817, vol. 1, no. ix, p. 670.

170 HRA, *Wylde to Macquarie*, 17 November 1817, vol. 1, no. ix, p. 671.

171 HRA, *Wylde to Macquarie*, 24 November 1817, vol. 1, no. ix, p. 676.

172 HRA, *Antill to Dewar and Busteed*, 1 December 1817, vol. 1, no. ix, pp. 691–2.

173 HRA, *Busteed to Antill*, 2 December 1817, vol. 1, no. ix, p. 692.

174 HRA, *Dewar to Campbell*, 1 December 1817, vol. 1, no. ix, p. 692.

175 See chapter one.

176 *Sydney Gazette and New South Wales Advertiser*, 27 December 1817.

177 HRA, *Macquarie to Bathurst*, 12 December 1817, vol. 1, no. ix, p. 561.

178 HRA, *Macquarie to Bathurst*, 12 December 1817, vol. 1, no. ix, p. 561.

179 Gregory Durston, *The Admiralty Sessions, 1536–1834: Maritime Crime and the Silver Oar* (Cambridge Scholars: 2017), p. 1.

180 Gregory Durston, *The Admiralty Sessions*, p. 7.

181 *Morning Chronicle*, 12 January 1819.

182 W.P. Courtney, *Oxford Dictionary of National Biography*, 'Sir Christopher Robinson' www.oxforddnb.com.proxy.lib.ul.ie/ view/article/23833 29 October 2017.

183 The Edinburgh Annual Register for 1819, Vol. Twelfth – Parts 1 and II (Edinburgh 1823), p. 52.

184 *The Times*, 12 January 1819.

185 *Morning Chronicle*, 12 January 1819.

186 *The Times*, 12 January 1819.

187 *The Times*, 12 January 1819.

188 *Morning Chronicle*, 12 January 1819.

189 *Morning Chronicle*, 12 January 1819.

190 *Morning Chronicle*, 12 January 1819.

191 *Morning Chronicle*, 13 January 1819.

192 *Morning Chronicle*, 13 January 1819.

193 *Morning Chronicle*, 13 January 1819.

194 *Morning Chronicle*, 13 January 1819.

195 *Morning Chronicle*, 13 January 1819.

7 *After the* Chapman

196 *Morning Chronicle*, 13 January 1819.

197 *Truth*, 7 November 1954.

198 Macintyre, *A concise history of Australia*, p. 48.

199 Report from the Select Committee on Transportation, 1812, p. 13.

200 Report from the Select Committee on Transportation, 1812, p. 13.

201 Report from the Select Committee on Transportation, 1812, p. 13.

202 HRA, Maule to Hobhouse, 19 January 1819, vol. 1, no. x, p. 145.

203 HRA, Hobhouse to Goldburn, 29 January 1819, vol. 1, no. x, p. 144–5.

204 HRA, Bathurst to Macquarie, 12 April 1819, vol. 1, no. x, p. 144.

205 East India Company & Civil Service Pensions, Popular Fund pension register, Abel Chapman reference, August 1835, L–MAR–C–833.

206 Convict Muster, *Chapman*, 2 August 1817.

207 *Sydney Morning Herald*, 19 April 1847.

208 *Maitland Mercury and Hunter River General Advertiser*, 18 September 1847.

209 *Maitland Mercury and Hunter River General Advertiser*, 18 September 1847.

210 *Bell's Life in Sydney and Sporting Reviewer*, 2 October 1847.

211 *Sydney Chronicle*, 6 November 1847.

212 For analysis of the decline in convict transportation to New South Wales see Rober Hughes, *The Fatal Shore* (London, 2003)

213 All statistical date pertaining to the number of ships and convicts leaving Ireland for New South Wales is extracted from *The convict ships, 1787–1868*, by Charles Bateson. 2nd ed. 1974.

214 Report of the Inspectors General of Prisons in Ireland, 1823, p. 11.

215 Report of the Inspectors General of Prisons in Ireland, 1824, p. 13.

216 Report of the Inspectors General of Prisons in Ireland, 1826, p. 42.

217 Report of the Inspectors General of Prisons in Ireland, 1829, p. 51.

218 House of Commons, Return in detail of the expense of the convict department at the Port of Cork, 1835, p. 6.

219 House of Commons, Return in detail of the expense of the convict department at the Port of Cork, 1835, p. 6.

220 John Dunmore Lang, 'Transportation and Colonization', *The British and Foreign Review; or European Quarterly Journal*, 5 (July–Oct 1837), p. 116.

221 'Chapman Voyages to Australia', Convict Records, https://convictrecords.com.au/ships/chapman (accessed 11 November 2017).

8 Conclusion

222 *The Sydney Gazette and New South Wales Advertiser*, 4 November 1826.

223 David Richards, 'Transported to New South Wales: medical convicts 1788–1850', *British Medical Journal*, 295 (19–26 December 1987), 1612.

224 Richards, 'Transported to New South Wales', p. 1610.

225 *Truth*, 7 November 1954.

226 *Truth*, 7 November 1954.

227 Cited in Leonard F. Gutteridge, *Mutiny: a history of naval insurrection* (Maryland, 1992), p. 5.

228 *Chapman*, transportation register, 1817.

229 *Truth*, 7 November 1954.

230 The Edinburgh Annual Register for 1819, twelfth volume – Parts I and II (Edinburgh, 1823), p. 53.

231 National Archives of Ireland, Chief Secretary's Office Registered Papers, Thomas Ryan to Lord Lieutenant, 8 December 1817.

232 *Truth*, 7 November 1954.

233 The Edinburgh Annual Register for 1819, twelfth volume – Parts I and II (Edinburgh, 1823), p. 52.

234 *Truth*, 7 November 1954.

235 *Chapman*, Convict Muster, 2 August 1817.

236 *Truth*, 7 November 1954.

237 *Truth*, 7 November 1954.

238 NAI, CSORP, Thomas Ryan to Lord Lieutenant, 8 December 1817.

239 The two most detailed accounts of this incident conflict as to whether the men were the alleged ringleaders.

240 NAI, CSORP, Thomas Ryan to Lord Lieutenant, 8 December 1817.

241 John McDonald and Ralph Shlomowitz, 'Mortality on Convict Voyages to Australia, 1788–1868', *Social Science History*, 13, 3 (Autumn, 1989), 300.

242 McDonald and Shlomowitz, 'Mortality on Convict Voyages to Australia', 287–9.

243 McDonald and Shlomowitz, 'Mortality on Convict Voyages to Australia', 302.

244 O'Toole, *The History of Australian corrections*, p. 25.

245 An Account of the number of convicts who have died in their passage to New South Wales since 1810 (Transport Office, London) 25 April 1816.

246 Leonard F. Guttridge, *Mutiny: a history of naval insurrection*, (Maryland, 1992), p. 5.

247 Guttridge, *Mutiny*, p. 5.

248 Guttridge, *Mutiny*, p. 5.

249 Susan Ballyn, 'Brutality versus common sense', p. 34.

250 Ballyn, 'Brutality versus common sense', p. 41.

251 Guttridge, *Mutiny*, p. 5.

252 Guttridge, *Mutiny*, p. 11.

Appendix 2

253 Blank spaces are present either because the original document is completely illegible or has been left blank. Some names and spelling will differ from those that may appear elsewhere in the book but they have been reproduced 'as found', wherever they have been encountered in original documents or newspaper reports.

Appendix 4

254 This is the best available list of *Chapman* convicts granted certificates of freedom. It is unlikely to be an exhaustive list, however, as there are approximately 140–50 men unaccounted for. Nor is it clear if the occupations listed here are those claimed by the convict when he arrived in 1817 or at the time of the granting of the certificate. It is important to note that occupations are self-declared by the convict so when an individual presents as a lawyer, it may have a slightly different meaning, such as, he may have been a clerk and is exaggerating his status.

Select Bibliography

Books

Adams, Robert, *Prison Riots in Britain and the USA* (Macmillan, 1994).

Bateson, Charles, *The Convict Ships* (London, 1974).

Binney, Keith Robert, *Horsemen of the First Frontier: 1788–1900 and the Serpent's Legacy* (Volcanic: Sydney, 2005).

Black, John, *An Authentic Narrative of the Mutiny on Board the Ship Lady Shore; with Particulars of a Journey through Part of Brazil* (London, 1798).

Brown, Kevin, *Poxed and Scurvied: The Story of Sickness and Health at Sea* (London, 2010).

Campbell, Malcolm *Ireland's New Worlds: Immigrants, Politics and Society in the United States and Australia, 1815–1922* (Wisconsin, 2008).

Carey, Tim, *Mountjoy: The Story of a Prison* (The Collins Press: Cork, 2000).

Durston, Gregory, *The Admiralty Sessions, 1536–1834: Maritime Crime and the Silver Oar* (Cambridge Scholars: 2017).

Emsley, Clive, *Crime, Police, and Penal Policy: European Experiences 1750–1940* (Oxford University Press: Oxford, 2007).

Foxhall, Katherine, *Health, Medicine, and the Sea* (Manchester, 2016).

Gutteridge, Leonard, F., *Mutiny: A History of Naval Insurrection* (Maryland, 1992).

Hughes, Robert, *The Fatal Shore* (London, 2003).

Inglis, Henry D., *Ireland in 1834: A Journey Throughout Ireland During the Spring, Summer and Autumn of 1834* (Whittaker and Co.: London, 1834).

Johnston, Helen, *Crime in England 1815–1880: experiencing the criminal justice system* (London, 2015).

Kavanagh, Joan and Dianne Snowden, *Van Diemen's Women: H history of Transportation to Tasmania* (The History Press Ireland: Dublin, 2015).

MacDonald, Janet, *The British Navy's Victualling Board, 1793–1815: Management Competence and Incompetence* (The Boydell Press: Woodbridge, 2010).

Macintyre, Stuart, *A Concise History of Australia* (Cambridge, 2006).

Morgan, Kenneth, *The Birth of Industrial Britain: Social Change, 1750–1850* (Pearson: London, 2004).

O'Toole, Seán, *The History of Australian Corrections* (University of New South Wales Press, 2006).

Quigley, Christine, *The Corpse: A History* (McFarland & Company: Jefferson, 1996).

Reid, Thomas, *Two Voyages to New South Wales and Van Diemen's Land with a Description of the Present Condition of that Interesting Colony* (Longman, London: 1822).

Tyner, George, *The Traveller's Guide through Ireland being an Accurate and Complete Companion to Captain Alexander Taylor's Map of Ireland* (Byrne: Dublin, 1794).

Articles, Chapters and Papers

Ballyn, Susan, 'Brutality versus Common Sense: the 'mutiny ships', the *Tottenham* and the *Chapman*' in Anna Haebich and Baden Offord (eds), *Landscapes of exile: once perilous, now safe* (Oxford, 2006), pp. 31–42.

Brasier, Angeline, 'Prisoners' bodies: methods and advances in convict medicine in the transportation era', *Health and History*, 12, 2 (2010).

Costello, Con, 'The convicts: transportation from Ireland' in Colm Kiernan (ed.) *Australia and Ireland 1788–1988: bicentenary essays* (Gill and Macmillan: Dublin, 1986).

Fletcher, Brian, 'Lachlan Macquarie' in David Clune and Ken Turner (eds), *The governors of New South Wales 1788–2010* (The Federation Press: Sydney, 2009).

Foxhall, Katherine, 'From convicts to colonists: the health of prisoners and the voyage to Australia, 1823–53', *The Journal of Imperial and Commonwealth History*, 39, 1 (March 2011), 1–19.

Gillespie, James Edward, 'The transportation of English convicts after 1783', *Journal of the American Institute of Criminal Law and Criminology*, 13, 3 (1922).

Hirst, John, 'The Australian experience: the convict colony' in Norval Morris and David J. Rothman (eds) *The Oxford History of the Prison: the practice of punishment in western society* (Oxford University Press: Oxford, 1998).

Humphrey, Kim, 'A new era of existence: convict transportation and the authority of the surgeon in colonial Australia', *Labour History*, 59 (November, 1990).

Karskens, Grace, 'Revisiting the worldview: the archaeology of convict households in Sydney's Rocks neighbourhood', *Historical Archaeology*, 37, 1 (2003).

Kercher, Bruce, 'Perish or prosper: the law and convict transportation in the British empire, 1700–1850, *Law and History Review*, 21, 3 (Autumn, 2003).

Lewis, Frank, 'The cost of convict transportation from Britain to Australia, 1796–1810', *The Economic History Review*, 41, 4 (November, 1988).

Maxwell-Stewart, Hamish, 'The rise and fall of penal transportation' in Paul Knepper and Anja Johansen (eds) *The Oxford Handbook of Crime and Criminal Justice* (Oxford University Press, Oxford: 2016).

Maxwell-Stewart, Hamish, 'Those lads contrived a plan: attempts at mutiny on Australia-bound convict vessels', in *International Review of Social History* (September 2013).

McDonald, John and Ralph Shlomowitz, 'Mortality on convict voyages to Australia, 1788–1868', *Social Science History*, 13, 3 (Autumn, 1989).

Richards, David, 'Transported to New South Wales: medical convicts 1788–1850', *British Medical Journal*, 295 (19–26 December 1987).

Robbins, Bill, 'Governor Macquarie's job descriptions and the bureaucratic control of the convict labour process', *Labour History*, 96 (May, 2009).

Sullivan, C.W., 'Reconsidering the convict ships', *New Hibernia Review*, 12, 4 (Winter, 2008).

Willis, James J. 'Transportation versus imprisonment in eighteenth and nineteenth-century Britain: penal power, liberty and the state', *Law and Society Review*, 39, 1 (March, 2005).

Online

'Chapman Voyages to Australia', Convict Records, https://convictrecords.com.au/ships/chapman (accessed 11 November 2017).

Courtney, W.P., 'Sir Christopher Robinson' in *Oxford Dictionary of National Biography* www.oxforddnb.com.proxy.lib.ul.ie/view/article/23833 (accessed 29 October 2017).

Currey, C.H., 'Baronn Field' in *Australian Dictionary of Biography* http://adb.anu.edu.au/biography/field-barron-2041 (accessed 12 September 2017).

'Explore Archives and Maps', British Library,

http://searcharchives.bl.uk/primo_library/libweb/action/dlDisplay.do?docId=IAMS045-001114738&fn=permalink&vid=IAMS_VU2 (accessed 30 October 2017).

Holder, R.F., 'John Thomas Campbell' in *Australian Dictionary of Biography* http://adb.anu.edu.au/biography/campbell-john-thomas-1873 (accessed 31 August 2017).

Lohan, Rena, 'Sources in the National Archives for research into the transportation of Irish convicts to Australia 1791–1853 (www.nationalarchives.ie/topics/transportation/transp1.html) (accessed 11 July 2016).

McKay, R.J., 'Sir John Wylde' in *Australian Dictionary of Biography* http://adb.anu.edu.au/biography/wylde-sir-john-2822 (accessed 5 September 2017).

New South Wales and Tasmania, Australia Convict Musters, 1806-1849, www.ancestry.com (accessed on 28 April 2016).

British Parliamentary Papers and Reports

1817 (343) (Ireland). Report of the commissioners appointed by the Crown to investigate certain alleged abuses in the Convict Department at Cork; together with the evidence taken before them, p. 1.

House of Commons, Return in detail of the expense of the convict department at the Port of Cork, 1835.

Report from the Select Committee on Transportation, 10 July 1812, p. 3.

Report of the Inspectors General of Prisons in Ireland, 1823.

Report of the Inspectors General of Prisons in Ireland, 1824.

Report of the Inspectors General of Prisons in Ireland, 1826.

Report of the Inspectors General of Prisons in Ireland, 1829.

Convict and Transportation Records

Chief Secretary's Office Registered Papers.

Historical Records of Australia, vol. ix.

Historical Records of Australia, vol. x.

New South Wales, Australia, Convict Indents, 1788–1842.

New South Wales, Australia, Colonial Secretary's Papers, 1788–1856.

New South Wales, Australia, Convict Ship Muster Rolls, 1790–1849.

New South Wales, Australia, Certificates of Freedom, 1810–14, 1827–67.

New South Wales, Australia, Convict Registers of Conditional and Absolute Pardons, 1788–1870.

New South Wales, Australia, Tickets of Leave, 1810–1869.

The Edinburgh Annual Register for 1819, Vol. Twelfth – Parts I and II (Edinburgh 1823).

Newspapers

Belfast Newsletter

Bell's Life in Sydney and Sporting Reviewer

Dublin Evening Post

Exeter Flying Post

Freeman's Journal

Maitland Mercury and Hunter River General Advertiser

Morning Chronicle
Morning Post
Sydney Chronicle
Sydney Gazette and New South Wales Advertiser
Sydney Morning Herald
The Times
Truth

Index